to be returned on or before

THE AGE OF ENCHANTMENT

The Age of Enchantment

Beardsley, Dulac and their Contemporaries 1890–1930

Rodney Engen

DULWICH PICTURE GALLERY

SCALA

© This edition Scala Publishers Ltd 2007
© Text Dulwich Picture Gallery 2007

First published in 2007 by
Scala Publishers Ltd
Northburgh House
10 Northburgh Street
London EC1V 0AT, UK
www.scalapublishers.com

In association with
Dulwich Picture Gallery
Gallery Road, London SE21 7AD
www.dulwichpicturegallery.org.uk

Published on the occasion of the exhibition
'The Age of Enchantment: Beardsley, Dulac
and their Contemporaries 1890–1930' at
Dulwich Picture Gallery, London, from
28 November 2007 to 17 February 2008.

ISBN: 978-1-85759-523-9

Edited by Oliver Craske
Designed by Nigel Soper
Production Director: Tim Clarke
Printed in Italy
10 9 8 7 6 5 4 3 2

ACKNOWLEDGEMENTS

My grateful thanks go to the numerous individuals who
opened their homes and collections to me. As a result of
their enthusiasm this exhibition consists largely of works
unseen by the public, and for this I am most grateful.
They include: Ian MacPhail, Stephen Calloway, Colin
White, Rachel Moss, Dr Michael Barclay, Robin Greer,
Peter and Angela Astwood, Malcolm Hillier, Rachel
Campbell, Nina Lobanov-Rostovsky, Jeremy and Eski
Thomas, Kendra and Allan Daniel and Victor Arwas.
I would also like to thank the members of staff of the
various institutions listed in the catalogue whose works
augment many of the private collectors' pieces, and for
invaluable research assistance from Marina Henderson,
Michael Patrick Hearn, and as always daily support and
advice from Malcolm Hillier.

Finally, on an indulgent personal note, I must
mention that this catalogue was completed on a true 'Age
of Enchantment' island in the Caribbean. Just two and a
half miles across and far from the trials of modern life, its
exotic rain forest, tropical foliage and brilliant blue sea
were and remain as inspiring today as when it was first
discovered hundreds of years ago. I am proud to call it
my home.

RODNEY ENGEN
Saba, Netherlands Antilles

Page 2:
Aubrey Beardsley,
The Abbe (cat. 15)

Page 6:
Kay Nielsen,
'The Dancing Princesses' (cat. 124)

Page 8:
Edmund Dulac,
'Fairy-land' (detail of cat. 111)

Contents

Foreword by Ian Dejardin, Director, Dulwich Picture Gallery   6

Essay

The Age of Enchantment   8

'Beautiful Decadence' and The Cult of Beardsley   12
Enchanted Disciples   15
In Search of the Fantastic   21
The Age of Colour   25
'I Believe in Fairies'   26
The Glasgow School   27
Master Enchanters   30
The Enchantment of Nature   33
International Enchantment   35
Enchantment at Home   46
The Lure of Exotic Empire   48
Notes   51

Catalogue

The Age of Enchantment: Fantasy in Britain 1890–1930   52

The Lure of the Far East   52
The Aesthete's Peacock   54
The Age of Decadence   57
Exquisite and Precious Tales   66
In the Gothic Shadow of Beardsley   78
Fairyland Fantasy   89
The Glasgow School Artists   90
The Age of Enchantment   98
The Enchantment of Nature   108
International Enchantment   118
The Fantastic Ballets Russes   148
Enchantment at Home   151
The Lure of Exotic Empire   153

Selected Bibliography   155
Index   158

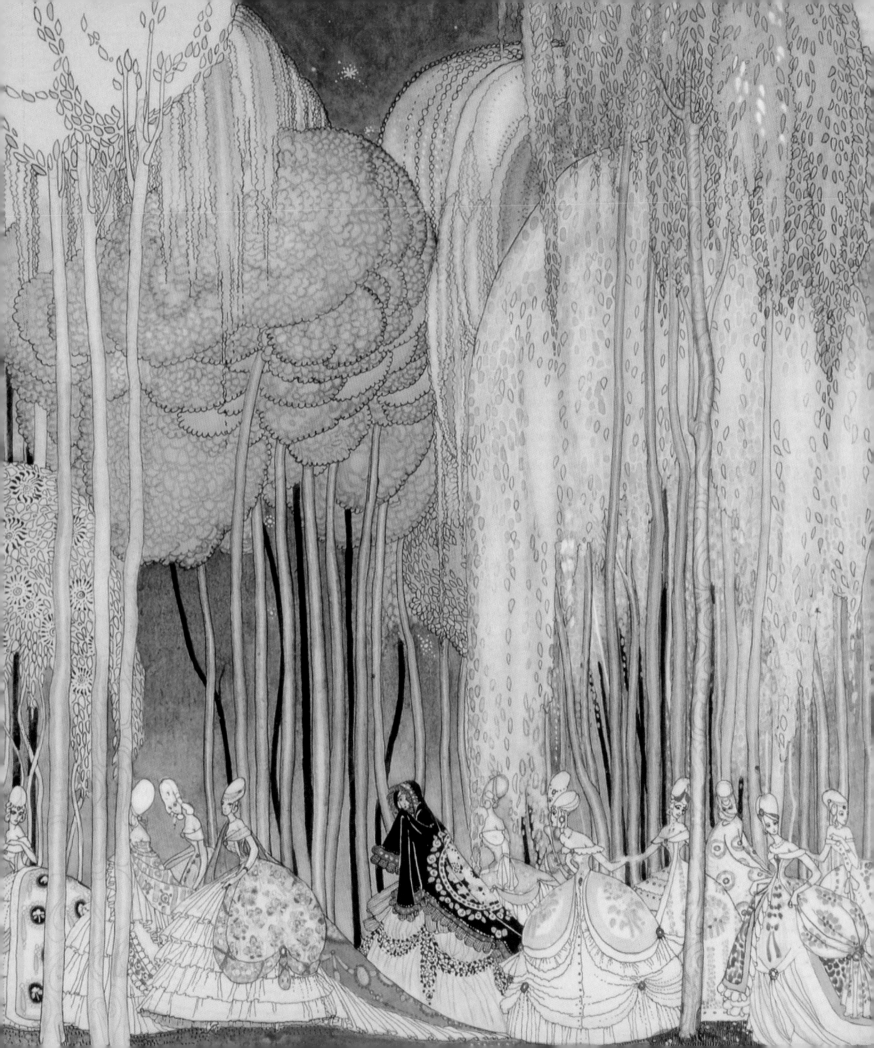

Foreword

*S*INCE 2001, DULWICH PICTURE GALLERY has organised a series of highly successful exhibitions devoted to British illustrators: E. H. Shepard, Arthur Rackham, William Heath Robinson and Beatrix Potter. All of these shows have made an important contribution to our understanding of the 'Golden Age' of book illustration in this country, perhaps quintessentially represented by the famous Arthur Rackham gift books produced before the First World War. This exhibition, curated by Rodney Engen, the scholar behind our memorable Rackham show and author of numerous books on this subject, follows a rather different path. Instead of focussing on one household name, this show looks at a particularly rich seam of illustration that was mined by many of the greatest illustrators of the age – producing what Rodney Engen has summed up in the title of the exhibition and this volume as an 'age of enchantment'. This was the fantasy storybook, typified by the eternal classic *Arabian Nights*. Finding its roots in the perversely beautiful work of Aubrey Beardsley, a whole genre of fantastic, swooningly exotic illustration blossomed – a hot-house bloom indeed. Rackham contributed his mastery of line and image; but the revelation here is that he was far from being the only master of the genre. The prodigious genius Edmund Dulac deserves an exhibition of his own; Kay Nielsen has just had one in his home country at the Holtegaard. And then there are Jessie King, Annie French, Alastair, the Detmold twins, Sidney Sime, and many, many others, all represented in this ravishing exhibition.

We owe Rodney Engen a real debt of gratitude for bringing this parade of astonishing talent together. He brings to life, in this catalogue, a whole era – one that seems far away from modern life, but whose imagery has fed into much that is familiar as well. How much of the visual language of *The Lord of the Rings* derives from J. R. R. Tolkien's familiarity with this period's illustration? Walt Disney was certainly influenced by it, so generations of children have imbibed at least a ghost of the original age of enchantment at the cinema. Names known for the most part only to specialists have their fascinating stories told – the tragic Detmold twins, the exotic Alastair.

The exhibition has been supported by the Robinson Bequest Fund and the Stanley Scott Fund; and most generously by the Friends of Dulwich Picture Gallery.

The show was organised by the exhibitions team at Dulwich Picture Gallery, Victoria Norton, Sanne Klinge and Mella Shaw, aided by Xavier F. Salomon, Curator of the Gallery.

We are also grateful for another fruitful collaboration with Scala Publishers, in particular Oliver Craske, and book designer Nigel Soper, who are responsible for the beauty of this catalogue.

IAN A. C. DEJARDIN
DIRECTOR, DULWICH PICTURE GALLERY

The Age of Enchantment

*'You can't shut out romance from the human heart;
you can't shut out wonder. And the romance and the
wonder of life will always find in Art an instrument
ready to hand. It may all be an illusion,
but if it is, so is life.'*

So wrote the artist Laurence Housman in *Pre-Raphaelitism in Art and Poetry* (1929). His remark echoes a sentiment which would dominate the culture of post-Victorian Britain. Once the aesthetic of High Victorian restraint and artistic repression, with its late undercurrents of decadence and sinful delight, had ceased upon the Queen's death, a new and more adventurous spirit slowly emerged in the arts and crafts of Britain. True, the so-called Edwardian Golden Age spawned a superficial, lavish and opulent aesthetic, but this was tempered by the horrors of World War One and its aftermath, when a war-weary public sought even more a new and more enchanted view of life. The nation yearned for escapist fantasy and turned in great numbers to the exotic tales and colourful designs which began to emerge in the arts of the new twentieth century. With this escapism came monumental changes in cultural attitudes towards art, literature, the theatre and music, architecture, decorative interiors and the many other necessities of a burgeoning middle class. The public's appetite veered away from the repressive High Victorian darkness towards colour, light and space – the very elements found on the continent and in the British Empire. As a result the populist medium of the lavishly illustrated gift book, filled with exciting escapist fantasies and devised by a new generation of artist-illustrators and designers, remains an especially fascinating barometer of that change. The artists and their influential works included here created a true 'Age of Enchantment'.

The turn-of-the-century artist-illustrator found the delights of fantasy and exoticism and a wonder of nature offered a refreshing antidote to the tenets of *fin-de-siècle* decadence. The latter had its own exciting and at times lascivious enticements, especially for a younger generation of artists determined to make their mark. These were largely associated with the scandalous drawings of the young renegade illustrator Aubrey Beardsley. This pale, slight, unprepossessing young artist and his delicate, provocative pen drawings came to represent the height of English decadence. With his friend Oscar Wilde and his artist disciples Charles Ricketts, Laurence Housman, Harry Clarke and Sidney Sime – all of whom initially embraced Beardsley's credo of decadence, sensuality and the fantastical with a schoolboy relish – they would set the pace for generations of influential artists. Even after Beardsley's premature death in 1898, when new signs of a healthier, less dark and more wholesome love of fantasy began to take hold, his influence survived well into the twentieth century. The results of this transformation into what has been called the 'Golden Age of Illustration', or more aptly 'The Age of Enchantment', are the subjects of the present book. It will explore this shift in public taste through the illustrations, books, decorative arts and ceramics of the period 1890–1930.

To understand how startling were the artistic contrasts between an age of decadence and an age of enchantment, one must first investigate the decadent age of Beardsley and ask just why his career held such powerful sway over his contemporaries. Many believed the key lay across the channel; British decadence took its inspiration from 'the poisonous honey of France', according to one contemporary critic. Experimentation was the keynote, as young British writers and artists believed in the demise of High Culture, just as the Queen was ending her long reign. They read and followed the decadent doctrines of Joris-Karl Huysmans and of Baudelaire, who claimed, 'The style of decadence is the ultimate utterance of the World – summoned to final expression and driven to its last hiding place.'

The British High Priest of Decadence was Oscar Wilde. His opponents believed his poetry, plays, novels and short stories were steeped in the heady scent of the abnormal, the sensual and the perverse. This attracted the young who were captivated by Wilde's devilishness. In his novel *The Picture of Dorian Gray* (1891), Wilde deliberately set out to scandalise: the novel's preface defiantly declared, 'There is no such thing as a moral or immoral book. Books are well written or badly written.' His main character, the beautiful and timelessly handsome Dorian Gray, describes the rapture he felt at reading the ultimate decadent novel, Huysmans's *À Rebours*, a book which lived up to its provocative title, embracing all things artificial and 'against nature', and provided the inspiration for generations of British aesthetes.

Thus emerged the British *fin de siècle*, with Wilde and Beardsley as its key exponents. Although the British strain of artistic decadence lacked the more obvious and (some would say) shocking characteristics seen by aesthetes visiting Paris, it did embrace anything visual or written which might confuse the reigning parameters of decency. Female emancipation shared a common platform with an outrageous fashion-consciousness, a moral lassitude depicted as overt eroticism, and a disturbing preoccupation with the grotesque and the mysteries of the spirit world, often cloaked respectably in classicism or at most a respect for eighteenth-century French excesses, notably the court of Louis XIV.

Just as communications dominate the twenty-first century, so too did the growth of various means of printed communication dominate Britain of the 1890s. In particular the rise of the popular illustrated press, the use of ambitious advertising methods, the rise of the poster as art form and the illustrated literary magazine followed by the more mainstream colour illustrated gift book, all nurtured by new printing technologies, helped to propagate a new aesthetic as well as establish the careers of many of the artist-illustrators and decorative designers represented here. The British middle classes were hungry for novelty and sophistication and, however ephemeral or unusual the period's productions, they had the money to sustain them. When Aubrey Beardsley edited *The Yellow Book*, that short-lived scandalous literary magazine which achieved notoriety overnight, the initial print run of 7,000 copies quickly sold out, and the magazine went into its fifth printing after just five months. Similarly *The Studio*, the first fine arts magazine seriously to investigate for its middle-class readership new book illustration and the decorative arts, was born. Beardsley in fact made his debut here when he designed *The Studio*'s cover; inside, its well-illustrated pages profiled the best new talents in the minor arts, which helped to earn its place as a taste-maker. Beardsley's rival Charles Ricketts started his own illustrated magazine, *The Dial*, which achieved a more rarefied following, steeped as it was in the tenets of French Symbolism, with contributions from many of the period's finest artists and writers.

Indeed publishing was the key to the propagation of the philosophy of decadence. A major figure in the publishing world of the 1890s was the enterprising publisher John Lane of the Bodley Head, and he eventually held the undisputed position as the man who made decadence pay – and handsomely. As the publisher of Beardsley, Oscar Wilde, Charles Ricketts and Laurence Housman, he had an astute eye for new talent and was a master of promotion. Noted for fanning the flames of controversy by publishing daring authors' works in rarefied limited editions, he sought to promote an air of exclusivity which greatly appealed to his sophisticated readership. His self-confessed 'passion for novelty' led to the production of slim volumes of exquisitely produced and designed books of vellum- or gilt leather-bound poetry, which led his critics to believe he only cared for presentation; he certainly pandered to an age of snobbish commercialism. He used Beardsley, Ricketts and Housman to help produce the image of the precious; it was not surprising that Wilde claimed Lane was the

Fig. 1: James McNeill Whistler's Peacock Room at the Freer Gallery of Art, Washington, DC inspired Beardsley in 1891.

purveyor of 'curious works of art'. Lane in fact rose to prominence in 1894 on the publications of Beardsley and Wilde, publishing Beardsley's designs to Wilde's *Salome*, and the same year Ricketts's designs to Wilde's *The Sphinx*, the latter limited to just 330 copies, priced at the princely sum of two guineas each.

Lane's authors and designers developed their distinctive approaches by emulating the French and going even further afield. They gathered in the cafés of London and Paris to exchange ideas and learn of the newest influences and movements. Japan had been an artistic magnet since it had been opened up to Western trade in 1853; by the 1870s, when the Arts and Crafts movement's bold, stark furniture designs emerged, it was clear the designers had embraced the oriental spare, minimal approach as a new and exciting direction. Artists like Whistler and illustrators like Walter Crane were quick to realise the potential of an oriental aesthetic: 'We have caught the vices of Japanese art certainly, even if we have assimilated some of the virtues,' recalled Crane, who became the primary exponent of Japanism

in book illustration after he had discovered Japanese woodblock prints used as wrapping paper.[1] This heralded the rise in 'things Japanese', from peacocks to lacquerware. Beardsley excitedly embraced its unconventional design elements, especially the exaggerated and shifted perspective so beloved by his French compatriots the Impressionists, once they too had adopted Japanism. 'Beardsley owned the most beautiful Japanese woodcuts one could see in London, all of the most detailed eroticism,' recalled one admirer. 'They were hanging in simple frames on delicately shaded wallpaper – all of them indecent, the wildest visions of Utamaro. Seen from a distance, however, they appeared very dainty, clever and harmless.'[2] In 1891 he visited James Abbott McNeill Whistler's celebrated Peacock Room interior, and came away further inspired by its imaginative orientalism (fig. 1). He produced a series of what he called 'Jap sketches', so anxious was he to claim Whistler as his intellectual property. By the 1900s the orientalist vogue proliferated to influence the decorative arts and especially furniture designed after Japanese and Chinese themes.

'BEAUTIFUL DECADENCE' AND THE CULT OF BEARDSLEY

THE LEGENDARY AUBREY BEARDSLEY was a phenomenon of his age. His extraordinary influence, which survives even today, is all the more remarkable since his own career lasted a mere six years, cut short by his untimely death at the age of 25. And yet he and his many devoted disciples are credited with revitalising the art and literature of late Victorian England. His work is very much aligned to his youthfulness, especially his gleeful regard for shocking and an obsessive attraction to the prurient. There was always a hint of rebelliousness about him: 'By the way, the goody-goody taste of the British public is somewhat peculiar. The very work that they expect from a French artist or author will only excite indignation if it emanates from the pencil or pen of an Englishman,' Beardsley wrote a year before his death. With his schoolboy antics and naive rhetoric he firmly believed his task was to shock a complacent British public, since 'the grotesque was the only alternative to insipid commonplace'.[3] In time, suffering from painful tuberculosis and knowing he would die young, he was determined to 'make his mark' and forced himself, sometimes through bouts of great pain, to embrace his chosen unconventional path right up to the end.

Beardsley was indeed a mythic character who at first sight appeared a harmless, rather frail-looking, androgynous youth (cat.7). But with his love of invention and a wicked sense of humour, a love of cosmopolitan literature and especially the theatre, he openly embraced the cult of decadence and turned its doctrines to his own purposes. Very rapidly he became in his public's mind the human embodiment of the decadent *fin de siècle*, a position he shared with Oscar Wilde (whom he later found repellent – ironically his association with Wilde was also to become the source of Beardsley's critical downfall). Indeed Beardsley drew himself as an elongated, gazelle-like, hatchet-faced boy. This was a calculated, naive image which hid a mind which many of his elder critics found repellent or simply immoral. A year before his death, when asked his opinion of his work to date, he explained, 'Of course, I think it's marvellously good,' he began with characteristic bravado, 'but if you won't think me beating about the bush, I may claim it as a proud boast that, although I have had to earn my bread and cheese by my hard work, I have always done my sketches, as people would say, "for the fun of the thing". No one had prescribed the lines on which I should work, or set any sort of limits on what I should do. I have worked to amuse myself, and if it has amused the public as well, so much the better for me! Of course I have one aim – the grotesque. If I am not grotesque I am nothing. Apart from the grotesque I suppose I may say that people like my decorative work, and that I may claim to have command of line. I try to get as much as possible out of a single curve or straight line.'[4]

Like many artists of his generation, Beardsley began his career as a copyist. Wholly self-taught, he found inspiration in such diverse sources as Kate Greenaway, the children's book illustrator, the Italians Mantegna and Botticelli, his champion Sir Edward Burne-Jones, and especially the Japanese print. An avid reader, he pored over exotic and rare volumes of poetry, drama, history and philosophy, and most of all his beloved French novelists like Balzac, while *Manon Lescaut*, *La Dame aux Camélias* and *Madame Bovary* were his favourite novels. But it was his reading of Huysmans's *À Rebours*, that 'breviary of decadence', which was to set the pattern of his life and art. As a treatise on decadence this one novel proved a revelation, while its main character, the aesthete Des Esseintes, became his alluring master. Even Oscar Wilde regarded the text as dangerously seductive, but the youthful Beardsley wholeheartedly embraced the philosophy of decadence described here in such exquisite detail and he willingly became its visual prophet. Here, according to Wilde, was 'the life of the senses as described in terms of mystical philosophy. One hardly knew whether one was reading the spiritual ecstasies of some medieval saint or the morbid confessions of a modern sinner. It was a poisonous book. The heavy odour of incense seemed to cling about its pages and to trouble the brain.' Consequently Wilde would in time turn against Beardsley and pronounce his decadent inventive drawings *fleurs du péché* (flowers of sin) which he likened to the addictive liquor absinthe: 'It's stronger than any other spirit and brings out the subconscious self in man. It is just like your drawings, Aubrey, it gets on one's nerves and is cruel… When I have before me one of your drawings I want to drink absinthe, which changes colour like jade in sunlight and makes the senses thrall, and then I can live myself back in imperial Rome, in the Rome of the later Caesars.'[5]

Although Beardsley's original pen and Indian ink drawings usually ended up photographed as process line block engravings, his extraordinary draughtsmanship can be seen in the originals shown here (cats 10, 11a, 11b, 12), which indicate they are the work of a master. He relished the cloak of secrecy he insisted upon while creating these miniature masterpieces and gleefully fuelled the myth that he worked only at night, by the light from his two favourite candlesticks. (He incorporated three candles in his monogram.) It was finally his first biographer, writing over ten years after his death, who pierced the veil of secrecy surrounding Beardsley's working methods: 'He sketched everything in pencil, at first covering the paper with apparent scrawls, constantly rubbed out and blocked in again, until the whole surface became raddled from pencil, india rubber, and knife: over this incoherent surface he worked in Chinese ink with a gold pen, often ignoring the pencil lines, afterwards carefully removed. So every drawing was invented, built up and completed on the same sheet of paper.' He also experimented with large areas of black ink, in contrast to the areas of the outline or the dense stipple dots he used in later drawings to emulate eighteenth-century French and Italian stipple engravings. Then there was what he called his 'black blot' method, a technique in which he would drop an inkblot onto the paper and move it about, then develop a plausible composition incorporating the element of chance into the composition. As a result his sharp eye for design allowed him to create some of the most strikingly bold and inventive black and white images ever produced.[6]

Beardsley's inventiveness surprised those who saw his early work. These included his early mentor Burne-Jones, the highly successful painter whom he and his actress sister had once visited at his studio in London. There the painter studied the young artist's early drawings and on their strength he encouraged Beardsley to pursue an artistic career. In fact Beardsley paid homage to his new mentor and champion when he borrowed from Burne-Jones's characteristic medievalism for the illustrations to his first public book commission. Indeed he produced a daunting number of ink drawings – over 300 small and full-page drawings – to J. M. Dent's edition of Malory's medievalist masterpiece, *Le Morte Darthur*, which appeared in 1894 (cats 11a–11b). Beardsley's approach, with large full-page drawings surrounded by ornate borders, each drawn in a mock-medieval heavy line to emulate early woodcuts, was an obvious crib from the Kelmscott Press publications of William Morris, and an outraged Morris pronounced the finished volume 'an act of usurpation' and threatened legal action. Beardsley, with the confidence of youth, remained unperturbed by Morris's criticism, which he dismissed in one rather arrogant sentence: 'The truth is that his work is mere imitation of old stuff, mine is fresh and original.' It was an audacious bid for attention by a young, spirited illustrator and it worked. But these same high spirits led him quickly to explore a wider source of inspiration. He favoured the bizarre, which he found in the period's grotesquely illustrated diagrams in contemporary medical textbooks and transposed these into his remarkable *Bon Mots* illustrations of 1893. Here his fertile imagination took control and he created a series of extraordinary manic doodles of embryonic creatures with foetal heads and satyr-like legs. This one three-volume work emerged as a unique expression of his ability to invent and to shock; it was also an exercise in pre-Freudian eroticism, peopled with brooding predatory females, a disturbing incubus of eunuch-like dwarfs and memorable compositions of androgynous males suggestive of transvestism. Alternatively when, from 1894, he served as art editor and produced four covers for the new literary magazine *The Yellow Book*, he created a gallery of characters which cleverly stood out to grab the eye of the bookstall browsing public. Each cover was a bold, fantastically inventive design in pure black line and shape printed onto a bright yellow background cover. The one included here (cat. 10), in which a pair of Venetian revellers wander the dark streets at a Venetian Carnevale – one of them a grotesque woman, possibly a prostitute, holding a phallic candle to highlight her corpulence – is a masterstroke of decadent design. In other works he created scenes with courting couples drawn in compromising positions which were so disturbing even to his publisher John Lane that the latter felt it necessary to censor them. In other inventions Beardsley, a lover of the classics,

borrowed freely from the worlds of Greece and Rome, as in his title page design to Wilde's *Salome*, which depicted a large-breasted, male-endowed hermaphrodite, which again Lane felt it necessary to censor. Similarly his design for 'Venus Between Terminal Gods' of 1895 (cat. 14) received the same censorious treatment. And yet these classically-inspired drawings were seemingly harmless to the uninitiated, and it was only after one searched the original version carefully and found the telling details that Beardsley created – his hermaphrodite's pronounced genitalia, giving them expertly drawn curves, and the figure's musculature so meticulously and anatomically correct – that one understands why they were considered shockingly real, and so they were censored.

Many consider Beardsley's illustrations to Oscar Wilde's *Salome*, published by John Lane in 1894, to be his masterpiece; *The Studio* magazine declared it 'the very essence of the decadent *fin de siècle*'. Here he incorporated all his favourite influences, from Greek vase painting, classical art and sculpture to Japanese prints, which he combined with a contemporary fluidity of line unique to the period. Wilde, however, was not pleased, especially since the waggish Beardsley had wickedly parodied the author as a corpulent, unsavoury character in the backgrounds of several works. He dismissed the drawings as 'not Byzantine' enough and 'too Japanese' and damned them rather perceptively as 'the naughty scribbles a precious schoolboy makes in the margins of his copybook'. Beardsley was upset but philosophical; he declared wearily that 'beauty is so difficult'. In fact he suffered further censorious insults from his publisher, when the nudity in his 'Enter Herodias' drawing (now in Princeton Library) was considered too accurate for popular taste and the drawing was dropped. He quipped in its margin: 'Because one figure was undressed / This little drawing was suppressed / It was unkind, but never mind, / Perhaps it all was for the best.' And yet upon publication Beardsley's version of Wilde's *Salome* contained more overtly erotic drawings in one book than had ever before been published and distributed in England (cat. 12).

When Beardsley's health was good, he could be prolific. Under his art editorship, *The Yellow Book* presented some of the most daring and influential works of illustration and literature of the period. Beardsley not only provided designs himself but he also commandeered works from his artist friends like Laurence Housman and, in a nod toward respectability, he secured contributions from the more serious old guard artists like Sir Frederic Leighton, although Leighton would eventually consider as ill-judged his early contribution and associations with the *Yellow Book* decadents, especially once a staid *Times* critic had declared *The Yellow Book* 'a combination of English rowdyism with French lubricity'. But, despite its critics, the short-lived *The Yellow Book* (which lasted a mere thirteen issues) provided a heady cocktail of provocative end-of-the-century decadence. 'Who wants these fantastic pictures?' asked the outraged critic of the *New York World*, who found Beardsley's imaginative drawings totally unacceptable, 'like Japanese sketches gone mad, of a woman with black tuft for a head, and snake-like fingers starting off the keyboard of a piano; of Mrs Patrick Campbell with a sticking-plaster hat, hunchy shoulders, a happily impossible waist, and a yard and a half of indefinite skirt… Then for the letterpress how little there is to be said. Mr Henry James in his most mincing mood; a Mr Beerbohm, whose "Defence of Cosmetics" contains… pure nonsense.'[7]

It was Beardsley's desire to shock which would prove his eventual downfall. By the late 1890s he was coupled in his public's minds with the now disgraced Oscar Wilde and together they were seen as threats to public respectability. Indeed Beardsley was removed from his position as art editor of *The Yellow Book* in 1895 largely because of his unsavoury associations. This was the period when he and his sister had bought their first house in Pimlico and filled it with decadent furnishings, including the desk displayed here (cat. 9). Strangely, however, it is in the work of this later period of Beardsley's career, from 1895 to 1898, that he produced the intricate masterpieces that transcend the mere schoolboy prankishness of his early years, imbuing his drawings with an exuberance, a masterful finish and a more detailed excellence – even experimenting with pencil shading and wash to accommodate the photoengraver. These remain some of his most influential illustrations and spawned a devoted school of artistic disciples. Some of these works were his contributions to the new literary magazine *The Savoy*, another short-lived but innovative publication, which survived a mere eight issues until it was banned by that ever-vigilant guardian of morals, the bookseller W. H. Smith. Beardsley created some of his most intricate and beautiful drawings for *The Savoy*, especially those with elaborately stippled surfaces in imitation of eighteenth-century engravings.

Then followed the equally dense and intricate costume drawings for an 1896 edition of Alexander Pope's *The Rape of the Lock*, a work which was so inventive and striking it inspired imitation by his later disciples. That same year his shocking masterpiece of classical eroticism appeared – Aristophenes's *Lysistrata*; but with its drawings of inflated phalluses and overt sexuality he later, as a Catholic convert, deeply regretted the exercise.

Gradually his style refined, and the areas of spare, almost oriental black and white spaces were filled with a myriad of tiny dots or later areas of wash to indicate texture and shape. He loved the exuberance of the seventeenth and eighteenth centuries' gowns and high wigs. They culminated in a series of elaborate drawings to an edition of Theophile Gautier's *Mademoiselle de Maupin*, whose cross-dressing heroine was a favourite of fellow decadents: Swinburne called Gautier's novel his 'Golden Book'; Baudelaire revered it, while Oscar Wilde never travelled without a copy. For his version Beardsley turned, rather appropriately, to mauve-tinted watercolour for the book's frontispiece and used a subtle, delicate grey wash for other drawings (cat. 18). Many of these were done during bouts of ill health as he suffered the pain and debilitation of severely congested lungs. At times he became so 'utterly cast down and wretched' that he couldn't work, especially upon the much-anticipated illustrations to a projected edition of Jonson's *Volpone* which he longed to complete

(cat. 17). He persevered slowly and these were to be his last drawings, painstakingly drawn during a forced recuperation at Menton.

And it was at Menton that Beardsley died on 16 March 1898 (cat. 8). It was a tragic loss to the world of illustration and heralded the dawn of a new and more tolerant Edwardian Age. But even from beyond the grave Beardsley's influence remained strong. While the voices of his many critics and admirers were quick to pass judgment upon his life and work, his publisher John Lane travelled to America where he spoke in New York in defence of his protégé, attempting to lend an air of respectability to his posthumous reputation: 'I said then, and repeat now, that he merely lashed out at the follies of his time, and that he had no more sympathy with decadence than Hogarth had for the vices depicted in *The Rake's Progress* and *Marriage à la Mode*. Knowledge must never be confounded with sympathy. I will go further, and declare that Beardsley, by his grotesque and powerful pictures of several tedious phases of life, dealt a death blow to decadence.'[8] There were many admirers, from students to professional artists, and they helped to confirm Beardsley's place in history: once Gabriel de Lautrec, that master of the earthy and the enigmatic, had written to Beardsley requesting a recent book to help with an article he was writing 'summing up' Beardsley's career and influence in France. The young new generation abstractionists Picasso, Kandinsky and Klee looked upon him as the creator of daring, precise abstractions and they remained devoted disciples. Later still Sergei Diaghilev, with his designer Leon Bakst, presented Beardsley-inspired sets and costumes for his innovative Ballets Russes productions.

And yet to the end Beardsley surrounded his work with mystery; even in his only known interview, given to *The Idler* magazine a year before his death, his answers to probing queries remained coy and defensive. Perhaps it was all an act after all, for Beardsley was above all a master publicist who was supremely adept at coping with and manipulating a burgeoning celebrity press.

The posthumous, so-called 'Beardsley Boom' was a short-lived yet intense phenomenon. According to his great admirer, the caricaturist Max Beerbohm, it was not long before forgeries and imitations abounded: 'It looked so simple and easy – a few blots and random curves, and there you are. Needless to say the results were appalling. But Beardsley was always, in many ways, developing and modifying his methods, and so was always ahead of his apish retinue.'[9] Six years after Beardsley's death, John Lane wrote that 'evidence is not wanting to show that his following is both enthusiastic and loyal. This applies not only to Great Britain, but equally to America, whilst in Germany, France, Belgium, Russia and Holland, it is safe to affirm his reputation is steadily growing, especially in Germany.'[10] And yet his detractors were many. Roger Fry damned Beardsley as 'the Fra Angelico of Satanism'; Beardsley's *New York Times* obituary pronounced him, 'incapable of creating anything belonging to a higher and a better art. His influence lowered taste and did not elevate it… The grotesque and the bizarre, being the unnatural and the abnormal, never can be made to live… A coming age will wonder why there was any brief interest taken in Beardsley's work. It was a passing fad, a little sign of decadence and nothing more.' Beardsley once countered such prudishness by asking, 'Have you ever noticed that it is the realism of one age which becomes the decorative art of the next?' The staunch Catholic poet and essayist Alice Meynell simply did not like Beardsley; five years after his death she continued her attacks: he 'never sets himself to arrange, to balance, to fill his corners, to weigh his blocks, to sweep the fine line, without busying his imagination to express an infernal evil – not, needless to say, passion or any of the ardours, but explicit evil standing alone.'[11] D. H. Lawrence used the discovery of Beardsley's *Salome* illustrations as the perfect emotional vehicle for one of his sexually confused characters in his first novel *The White Peacock* (1911), when his protagonist finds a satisfying yet unexplainable elation in studying the drawings: 'I sat and looked and my soul leaped out upon the new thing. I was bewildered, wondering, guessing, fascinated. I looked a long time, but my mind, or my soul, would come to no state of coherence. I was fascinated and overcome, but yet full of stubbornness and resistance.'[12]

Today Beardsley is looked upon as a true precursor of the Modern Age, a pioneering inventor of abstractionism whose career rose upon the crest of a populist wave – the so-called cult of 'ego-mania' of which he represented a supreme example of the 'uncontrollable genius'. Along with Oscar Wilde, he had perfected what one impassioned contemporary German critic described in his bestselling, highly-charged study *Degeneration* (which was widely read when translated into English in 1895) as 'the ego-mania of decadentism, its love of the artificial, its aversion to nature and to all forms of activity and movement, the megalomaniacal contempt for men and its exaggeration of the importance of art, have found their English representatives among the "Aesthetes", the chief of whom is Oscar Wilde.'[13]

ENCHANTED DISCIPLES

EANWHILE BEARDSLEY'S numerous disciples carried his decadent torch well into the new century. One of the most talented was Laurence Housman, who was also a friend and confidante of Oscar Wilde. Indeed, only a few months after Beardsley's death a broken Wilde, then living in French exile following his imprisonment, gratefully received a letter of comfort from Housman. Wilde was clearly flattered by the attentions of the young Housman and responded effusively: 'Style is certainly part of your character; your soul has beautiful curves and colours.' Here too Wilde told Housman that the secret to the coming century's new artistic horizons lay within the colourful world of the exotic, and how he planned to decamp to a small village near Cannes ('I am to write there!') to create 'a work of art' inspired by the heady atmosphere of the South: 'The high sapphire wall of sea, the gold dust of the sun, the petals and perfumes of southern flowers – perhaps these may tune my soul to some note of beauty.'[14]

Laurence Housman

Laurence Housman (fig. 2) had a great affinity with the Beardsley–Wilde circle, and began his career steeped in their decadent philosophy. Born on 18 July 1865 at Perry Hall, Bromsgrove, Worcestershire, one of seven children (his elder brother was the celebrated poet A. E. Housman), Laurence was a precocious child with a vivid imagination and a lifelong love of fairy tales and legends. Determined to escape the confines of his rural environment at an early age, he and his devoted sister Clemence left home in 1883 for the seductive trials and uncertain challenges of artistic life in London. Laurence was then just eighteen. They enrolled in the City and Guilds Art School in South Lambeth, where Laurence studied drawing

Fig. 2: Laurence Housman.

for commercial illustration and Clemence quickly perfected the wood engraving technique to be able to interpret her brother's drawings for publication. Laurence soon moved on to the South Kensington Art School and began to search out illustration commissions which, being a natural illustrator, he secured easily. These first illustrations had to be drawn upon small, hard boxwood blocks in pen and ink, each minute pen line then meticulously engraved by Clemence; later he used chalk on card and paper for photographic reproductions.

At this time it was Clemence who supported them both by wood engraving commissions, while Laurence struggled to find a distinctive voice in the competitive world of book and magazine illustration. He read avidly and borrowed from his favourites, like William Blake and the Sixties School of Victorian illustrators, whom he later wrote about and championed. In 1894 Beardsley's enterprising publisher John Lane (who had 80 titles in his list at the time) approached Housman for a contribution. Lane shared with Laurence the absolute belief in the book as an art form: its design had to be an artistic marriage of binding, typeface, layout and illustration. At this time Housman had befriended another Lane artist, Charles Ricketts, from whom he learned a great deal about book design. It was in fact Ricketts, he later explained, who 'dropped me away from my timid preference for fuzzy chalk drawing, as a means of concealing my bad draughtsmanship, and had set me to pen-work, with Rossetti and other Pre-Raphaelites as my main guides both in composition and technique. From that time on I felt set – I acquired a new confidence; I had found at last what I wanted to do.'[15]

Their relationship soon foundered and Housman's visits to The Vale (Ricketts' Chelsea house, which he shared with his partner, the artist Charles Shannon) turned into critical ordeals, 'a zigzag course of acceptance and escape', which upset more than helped the impressionable Housman. However it was Ricketts's influence which permeated the ten book illustration commissions Housman completed for Lane over the next ten years. Indeed, he became an outspoken exponent of the inventive book format, reviving the tall elegant shapes he found in medieval models. He always insisted upon complete control over a book's format and design from the very beginning: it was 'as unreasonable to expect a designer always to design with a set format as it would be to expect a painter to paint with a frame of a fixed size and shape'. Working for Lane proved excessively demanding, and while Housman accepted his tasks, not only drawing and designing but superintending the books through the presses, making arrangements for binding materials and even inks, he found each project unnecessarily constricting and ultimately frustrating. A perfectionist, he chose all materials carefully, from quirky bindings of varnished wrapping paper to a 'dress material' of coarse-grained linen (cat. 21).

But it was book illustration which most interested Housman, who not only practised it, but also studied its history and wrote about and championed its finest historical exponents. He is in fact credited with reviving interest in unjustly neglected illustrators: he wrote several books

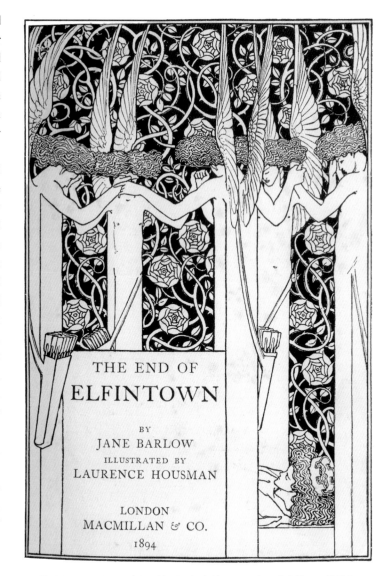

Fig. 3: Laurence Housman's Beardsley-inspired title page to *The End of Elfintown* (1894).

and articles for respected magazines on his favourites, like the Sixties School practitioners Arthur Boyd Houghton and Arthur Hughes. He insisted that the true illustration 'becomes not what we so often find, the dull repetition, through another medium of things already sufficiently made clear by the text; but something new with further appeals and fresh charms for the imagination… in a word, the result of another creative faculty at work on the same theme.'[16] His own teaching methods were self-discipline and structure: he found by making bookplate designs he could hone his compositional skills within the confines of a restricted space, and he completed at least fourteen for friends or patrons, each one a small jewel, with intricately attenuated figures, Celtic interlace, or simple but well-designed typography.

Housman created some of the finest illustrations of the late 1890s and his debt to Beardsley and Ricketts is unmistakable, especially in *The End of Elfintown* (fig. 3). Most notable was the group of drawings for

Fig. 4: Housman's goblins in *Goblin Market* (1893).

are bolder, their cat- and bird-like faces covered menacingly in voluminous cloaks and wide-brimmed hats of Beardsleyesque pen work. They were the products of a self-confessed 'freakish imagination' and even attracted the attention of the staid Sir Frederic Leighton, then President of the Royal Academy. Leighton, who in fact owned some of Beardsley's early drawings, admired Housman's concept and bought his original frontispiece drawing for the book: 'What struck him most in my work was the combination of figures with decoration,' Housman recalled. The authoress's verdict was less enthusiastic, and while she did not dislike Housman's treatment she explained, 'I don't think my Goblins were quite so ugly.'[17]

Housman shared Beardsley's renegade spirit, and created drawings which provoked or shocked by their overt illusions, often adopting themes of a perverted sexuality. As a result John Lane was forced to emulate the censorship procedure once used for Beardsley's work to carefully investigate Housman's drawings, for Housman also liked controversy. (In later years he was dubbed 'the most censored playwright in Britain' for his irreverent and candid accounts of the royal family.) Lane often resorted to using a magnifying glass to search out any offensive nudity or veiled messages of a less than wholesome nature – which he did find. One rejected frontispiece of a group of sinewy male nudes suggestively posed alongside a stream (to illustrate 'The Reflected Faun' in Francis Thompson's *Poems*) was cheerfully recycled when it was accepted for the first issue of Beardsley's more daring *Yellow Book*. In time Housman was more willing to embrace his own homosexual nature, and he would openly fill his illustrations with veiled allusions to the homoerotic theme, much to the delight of Wilde and Beardsley. When Wilde emerged from jail in 1897, Housman sent him a copy of *All Fellows* (fig. 5), his recently published book of fantasy tales which he had freely filled with attenuated nudes and tortured figures (which coincidentally arrived with a copy of his brother's *A Shropshire Lad*) and elicited Wilde's comment, 'So you two brothers have between you given me a taste of that rare thing called happiness.'[18]

More to the point here, Laurence Housman was a fantasist, a poet and inventor or interpreter of the escapist fairy stories he illustrated. He did not totally share Beardsley's love of scandal, however, for Housman's was a refreshingly naive vision, positive and always moral, although sometimes grotesque in appearance, but always filled with wonderfully poetic, colour-inspired images – of strange beasts, of country folk lost to their fate – and a love of the bizarre and ultimately (being a religious man) the spiritual. Between 1894 and 1904 Housman produced a group of these tales in four separate volumes, which he illustrated and designed as well as wrote: *A Farm in Fairyland* (1894), *The House of Joy* (cat. 22), *The Field of Clover* (figs 6–7 and cats 24–25) and *The Blue Moon* (1904). Each successfully appealed to a new generation of fantasists; they were so popular they were later re-issued, published in extracts, and remain in print today. As early as 1907 Housman's retelling of tales from the *Arabian Nights* was illustrated with colour plates by Edmund Dulac, which helped to launch Dulac's own career as a fantasist. Each small,

Goblin Market, a project he initiated himself, after admiring Christina Rossetti's haunting poem, which had first been illustrated by her brother Dante Gabriel in 1862. Rossetti was at first unwilling to consent to further attempts at illustrations, but Housman persisted. He favoured a more medieval approach, and wrote to the poem's publisher George Macmillan with a series of rough sketches to suggest this approach. He believed the key to his success lay with the goblins, and he turned to Greek drama for inspiration: 'I have imagined goblins wearing animal masks in order to hide the wickedness that their faces would reveal; this will give me the opportunity of a dramatic climax when in the poem they are finally defeated by Lizzie. I propose then to show them throwing aside their masks as they make their escape.' The mask idea was rejected by the authoress, and while she consented to his illustrating her poem, he had to compromise over the 33 drawings of grotesque creatures he eventually completed (fig. 4). In tone they echo Dante Gabriel's earlier drawings, yet Housman's

Fig. 5: Housman's veiled homo-erotic illustrations in *All Fellows* (1896) unusually passed the censor.

Fig. 6: Housman's binding design for *The Field of Clover* (1898).

precious volume was densely illustrated by Housman in a mock-Pre-Raphaelite style which emphasised a deep whimsy as well as a disturbing claustrophobia. His figures filled every space; they stretched contorted through doorways or lay entwined within Nature. 'Mr Housman is strangely at home in fairyland. There is something distinctly uncanny about this obvious and serious familiarity with a place that is not a place "within the measure of the Act"', remarked one champion in 1908. Housman agreed: 'The true end and object of a fairy tale is the expression of the joy of living. There begins and ends the morality of the fairy tale: its value consists in its optimism. So for the true and unpolluted air of fairyland we have to go back to the old and artless tales of a day pure and simpler than our own, purer because so wholly unconcerned with any question of morals, simpler because so wholly unconscious of its simplicity.'[19]

The Times tried to explain how Housman could produce 'a long line of queerly original fairy tales, of which the sometimes queerer illustrations by himself were engraved by his sister Clemence'. They declared he was well qualified: 'He had a distinct fondness, even a passion, for freaks of psychology: to his friends it often seemed that his own mind was essentially freakish. Certainly many of his books carry introspective glimpses of his own soul of a disturbing oddity.' Housman preferred a more honest

explanation: 'Romantic in temperament, and religiously sentimental in my upbringing, I began by preferring things medieval to things modern; my poems, fairy tales, and legends were nearly all idealistic and fanciful – away from reality.'[20] He borrowed artistically from a variety of historical sources, such as Greek vase painting, Renaissance and Italianate architecture, Dutch interiors, a Germanic medievalism seen especially in his beloved Dürer, Pre-Raphaelite figures in long gowns set in intricate rural landscapes, as well as the exoticism of Beardsley and the French Symbolists.

Each volume was filled with full-page illustrations originally drawn in meticulous pen and ink line, dense, assured and rich. While his anatomy occasionally faltered, he compensated for this by mastering a drawing's overall composition, conscious that the format of the page directed the viewer's eye into the drawing. We do not know exactly how Housman worked, for he was never as forthcoming about his working methods as Beardsley. Those few pen and ink drawings and studies that survive (cats 22–25) were done with an almost infinitesimal fineness of line, drawn without the aid of a magnifying glass. Like Beardsley, he loved the immediacy of drawing in ink on paper or card: 'I think I have eyes at the tips of my fingers, I seem to feel the line even if I can hardly see it.' Those sketches for completed illustrations that do survive suggest a surprising boldness in ink or chalk, before he transferred them to wood block or

Fig. 7: 'The Passionate Puppets', the final published illustration in *The Field of Clover* (see cat. 25).

photoengraved page to hone away at the eventual jewel-like surfaces, much as the Pre-Raphaelite illustrators had done.

Eventually such fine work took its toll and brought on the debilitating poor eyesight which forced Housman to retire from illustration in favour of writing poetry and plays, which he did quite successfully until his death in 1959. His illustration career lasted a mere twelve years. He had over those years dabbled in poetry, and, although reticent to show his work to his more famous poet brother Alfred, he had published his first volume of verse, *Green Arras* in 1896, which he illustrated with five dense full-page drawings. This was the volume he had sent a much appreciative Oscar Wilde, then just out of prison. Subsequent volumes of verse, such as *All Fellows* (1896) and *Seven Legends of Lower Redemption* (1923) were filled with a religious fervour amid themes of evil and temptation; the former was a book he declared years later 'still has my heart'. But it was Housman's illustrations to Shelley's poem *The Sensitive Plant* (1898) which many consider his finest work of interpretive illustration. Here on delicately drawn plates, which were unusually photoengraved to a very high standard and printed on fine paper or vellum, he captured the delicacy of Shelley's world; in intricate stipple and elegant line, his draped classical figures are set within lush foliage and elaborate formal gardens. Housman explained how they were 'something technically in advance of anything I

Charles Ricketts, ARA

Of the associates of Beardsley presented here, Charles Ricketts (fig. 8) retained the closest link to his life and career: Ricketts always claimed his own illustrations were 'swamped forever by the success of Beardsley'. A fellow friend and interpreter of Wilde, who in fact illustrated or designed bindings for most of Wilde's books, Ricketts claimed Beardsley borrowed from him and soon turned bitter towards his successful rival: 'Beardsley, like Wilde, is typical of the decade which clothed its hedonism with brilliance, but also with the wish to astonish and "arrive".' And yet the prolific Ricketts, with over 80 books illustrated or designed during his lifetime, remains one of the most imaginative of Beardsley-styled artists.

There was in fact more to Ricketts than mere imitation. His long artistic career of over 50 years included successful forays into the fields of illustration, book design, wood engraving, painting, sculpture, theatrical design (his designs prefigured those of Bakst for the Ballets Russes) as well as connoisseurship and writing. True, he willingly borrowed from such diverse sources as the Old Master drawings, prints and paintings he and his partner the artist Charles Shannon spent their lifetime collecting. Ricketts eventually possessed an encyclopaedic knowledge of illustration, amassed from his habit of collecting whatever he favoured, from bundles of old cheap reproductions, to the Greek vases and gems, Egyptian antiquities, Persian miniatures and Japanese prints and drawings which eventually formed the core of one of the most celebrated private collections in Britain (it was later presented to the Fitzwilliam Museum, Cambridge). But Ricketts the illustrator arguably held a wider and more beneficial influence over the field than Beardsley: at the same time as Beardsley pursued just one aspect – pen and ink draughtsmanship – Ricketts insisted upon book design as an integral part of an illustrator's role. In the end, along with William Morris he remains one of the most influential founders of the private press movement in Britain.

Ricketts was an endearing individual, generous of spirit, who preached the 'cult of the exquisite' with a refined attitude towards the arts which many found stimulating. Oscar Wilde called him 'an orchid' and often visited his Chelsea home, the Vale, which he declared was 'the one house in London where you will never be bored'. Bernard Shaw saw him as 'the noble and generous Ricketts… a natural aristocrat as well as a loyal and devoted artist'. Born in Geneva on 2 October 1866, he eventually lived in London, although he was greatly drawn to France and Italy. A cosmopolitan childhood ended abruptly when he was orphaned at sixteen and apprenticed to a wood engraver in Lambeth, South London. There he met his lifelong partner Charles Shannon, and together they set about making a mark upon the artistic life of late nineteenth-century London.

Ricketts supported Shannon's painting career by illustrating for the period's numerous black and white magazines; it was artistic prostitution, which he called 'hack work', and later he bought up the originals of many of his early ink drawings to destroy after they had been photo-mechanically reproduced. But such money-spinners allowed him to explore and incorporate favourite themes from his historical studies. He was a superb pen draughtsman, his training in wood engraving giving him a firm mastery of the art of line, as well as concentrated detail, surface pattern, what he called 'filigree… an almost Persian finicky and finish', which like Housman he borrowed from the jewel-like surfaces of Pre-Raphaelite wood engravings. The result was exquisite pen work, like his early masterpiece 'Oedipus and the Sphinx' (1891; cat. 31). Here, borrowing from such diverse influences as Gustave Moreau, Dürer and Rossetti, he produced a masterpiece for Sir Frederic Leighton, who, like Beardsley before him, had commissioned the drawing for a standard fee of £5. Leighton pronounced the work of 'weird charm' and 'a marvellous piece of penmanship'. It remains one of the first Symbolist drawings in England, based as it was upon literary rather than mere artistic themes. Moreover, its ancient Greek subject, which had inspired Ingres as well as Moreau, was suggestive of the artist's own fixation with the struggle between man and his fate.[21]

As a book designer Ricketts was unparalleled. Unusually for the period, he adapted his designs to the tenor of the book; his elegant, understated line and overall purity of conception were unique. His designs for Oscar Wilde's *The Sphinx* (1894) are widely held to be his finest (cats 32–33). Given full control by Wilde over the book's design, format, illustration and type arrangement, he used rich materials, fine paper and a precious white vellum blocked in gold for the binding. He described his unorthodox approach: 'This is the first book of the modern revival of printing printed in red, black and green; the small bulk of the text and unusual length of the lines necessitated quite a peculiar arrangement; here I made an effort away from the Renaissance towards a book marked by surviving classical traits, printing it in Capitals.' Ricketts considered the illustrations his finest and most lyrical, although Wilde surprised him and did not agree: 'No, my dear Ricketts, [they] are not of your best. You have seen them through your intellect, not your temperament.' Ricketts attempted a timelessness, to 'evolve what one might imagine as possible in one charmed moment or place'. One recent critic found them totally successful to our modern eye: 'The drawings achieve this timeless rarefied atmosphere; they have a hieratic quality and the sense is conveyed of ritual action arrested at the very moment when the composition of the elements is perfect.'[22] Sadly the book was not a financial success: although ready for publication in 1893, it was postponed by John Lane for a year so as not to compete with Beardsley's *Salome*, which achieved a *succès de scandale*. Eventually a large number of the 200 printed copies remained unsold and these were destroyed in a fire in 1899 (along with its original woodblocks), to confer upon *The Sphinx* the dubious distinction of being not only the most precious but also among the rarest of Ricketts's books.

Nevertheless Ricketts was undeterred and he pursued his own Vale

Fig. 8: Charles Ricketts.

Press publications, from 1896 to 1904 producing, illustrating and printing over 80 titles, including a 37-volume edition of Shakespeare, which proved the press's swansong. He also designed a special type font, which he called the 'Vale'. His aim for the press was simple: 'A certain amount of fine literature, owing to its quality of permanence, suggests for that reason the desirability of a beautiful and permanent form for it.' The finest of the Vale publications are those in which Ricketts's own wood-engraved illustrations appeared throughout the text. A good example was his work for two versions of the 'Cupid and Psyche' story (English and Latin). Some designs suggest a lingering Pre-Raphaelite influence, others bow unashamedly towards Beardsley, especially in composition, despite being immersed in more classical settings (cat. 34).

With the closure of the Vale Press, and a waning interest in illustration and book design, Ricketts took up oil painting, sculpture, jewellery design and, most successfully, theatrical design. At first embarked upon light-heartedly as 'a holiday task', Ricketts's designs for the stage soon became influential and innovative, and, although begun at the late age of 40, they secured his name among some of the best designers for the stage. His love of Japanese art, especially Noh theatre, helped to inspire his conceptions. Between 1906 and 1931 he was involved in over 50 productions. Wagner loomed large and he was commissioned by the tenor Melchoir to design for

Bayreuth; in 1926 he produced designs for a production of *The Mikado* using stencilled Japanese patterns, which he painted single-handedly. As part of the design process he produced over the last 20 years of his life several hundred large watercolour designs for stage and sets. These have the finish and the considered compositions of fine paintings, and, while many productions never reached fruition, the paintings remain as valuable documents of a fertile imagination working in the robust 1920s Art Deco style (cats 136–137).

Some admirers linked him with the Ballets Russes designs of Leon Bakst, whom he greatly admired, but Ricketts, with characteristic modesty, explained to his champion Gordon Bottomley how his career was overshadowed by greater talents: 'No, my dear chap, the Russian designers owe me nothing. My book illustration work has been swamped for ever by the success of Beardsley – whom they know. My stage work, which anticipated much of theirs – the all-red Attila scene, the all-blue Salome… and countless details too long to describe, such as huge patterns and fantastic head dresses, are unknown to them; they are known here and remembered only by the theatrical profession. Any chance likeness you may detect lies in a common indebtedness to [Gustave] Moreau, or should I say to things initiated or discovered by Moreau; remains a certain local and semi-oriental element which is spontaneous and which with me is replaced by many complex currents of experience. Viewing my theatre work in relation to theirs, I should say that theirs is adventurous and lyric, and mine more intimate and tragic.'[23]

Finally there was a return to the fantastic, decorative elements in his later book designs, notably a second set of designs for Wilde's *The Sphinx*, and the five full-page illustrations for *Beyond the Threshold* (1929), which he completed two years before his death. The *Sphinx* designs adhere to a bolder compositional stance; his largely nude male and female figures are more sculptural, solid, rather than painterly. In others he used the silhouette technique of figure against solid background (cats 32–33). The five *Threshold* drawings illustrate a book of decadent dialogues written in the style of Wilde, to whom Ricketts was still devoted even after the writer's death. They hint at where his work may have taken him had he survived, the exquisite historicism he perfected transformed into a bolder more powerful modernity (cats 35–36). As Ricketts explained to the last: 'Art has been, Art is. So the present touches wings with the past.' He died in 1931, a much-loved artist, collector and designer, leaving a legacy of remarkable inventiveness which continues to inspire book, stage and decorative designers even today.

IN SEARCH OF THE FANTASTIC

Sidney Sime

ONE OF THE MORE EXTRAORDINARY DISCIPLES of Beardsley, who mastered his black and white world yet transformed it into a darker, more bizarre and thoroughly grotesque series of illustrations, was Sidney Herbert Sime (fig. 9). Of all the black and white illustrators in the Beardsley tradition, Sime was the most original. His life alone was quite remarkable, as his biographer once explained: 'He started out as a pit-boy, became a celebrity in the Nineties, collaborated with and became a close friend of two talented noblemen, and died poor and forgotten. Sime's life reads like a popular Victorian novel.' Born in Manchester in 1867, he worked as a youth in the Yorkshire coal mines for five years, immersed underground in an inky blackness which was to become his greatest inspiration. Here he practised scratching drawings of imps and devils upon the pit surface walls. He turned next to sign writing, then entered the Liverpool School of Art determined to become an artist. In 1893, aged 26, he moved to London, where at the same time the young Beardsley was hard at work on his *Morte Darthur* illustrations. It soon became clear to Sime at least that their artistic aspirations matched: 'After a while I realised that the only profitable life for a beginner was book illustrating.'[24]

He first began illustrating for a number of black and white process engraved magazines of the day, starting with such comic papers as *Pick-Me-Up*, then *The Idler*, *Eureka* and *Pall Mall Magazine*. For these he reported on current events; he especially loved the theatre and produced pen portraits of the period's finest actors, from Dan Leno to Sarah Bernhardt, who appeared in his regular feature 'Through the Opera Glass'. The more sophisticated paper *The Idler*, founded in 1892 by the novelist and playwright Jerome K. Jerome for 'people of artistic sympathies', published some of Sime's most striking illustrations from 1896, especially his 'Shades' series of ghostly wash-drawn political portraits, and the more bizarre classical themes 'The Great God Pan' (emulating Housman's favourite theme) and the Beardsleyesque 'The Mermaid' (cat. 38). These must have provided the printer with real challenges to reproduce in half-tones the subtlety inherent in Sime's original thin grey washes, charcoal or black ink, and lampblack highlighted in Chinese white. In fact Sime used whatever method or implement he felt would give the desired effect. Like Beardsley, he worked at night, often 'armed with a bulls-eye lantern and my paint-box, on the lookout for moonscapes'. He utilized brushes, pens, knives and even sponges in an attempt to create a variety of textures and atmospheres never before seen in black and white illustration.

One contemporary admirer felt, 'There is behind all Sime's work an extraordinary sense of one who has felt the immensity of life.' A curious, intensely serious figure, Sime insisted he 'was not posing' just because his works were difficult to understand. He merely sought inspiration from the grotesque: 'What I do I don't do consciously. I have a natural inherent bent towards mystery, and things must appear to be touched with what I may call the "bogey wand" or – well, I simply don't see them!'[25] A true disciple of Beardsley, Sime delighted in shocking, and when he became editor of the rather staid magazine *Eureka* in 1897 he attempted to transform its pages by producing his first truly Beardsley-inspired designs, which appeared from September. Here especially were two powerful pen works: 'The Mermaid', a portrait of an anguished figure crying out and engulfed by a bubbling wave, and 'The Felon Flower', intended to illustrate *The Legend of Mandrake*, a poem by Knight Ryder (cat. 37). Sime's rendition of the poem's couple cowering beneath a tree hung with a cadaverous body, the figure outlined in blackness, flapping in the breeze, is unforgettable. It accompanied the chilling verse:

> She eyes the flesh not yet begun to rot
> And screams a hollow laugh that evil bodes
> For lo! 'Twill simmer bravely in the pot
> When mixed with precious venom squeezed from toads.

With a large inheritance, Sime purchased *The Idler* in 1898, and as its new editor he set about transforming the magazine's image by using the decadent's violet and grey inks which replaced the more conservative black, red and cream of past issues. Here in 1899 he happily illustrated verses from favourite writers, like his version of Edgar Allan Poe's 'The Moon', which depicts a voluptuous female nude enveloped in a soft moonlight ('Over every drowsy thing – And buries them up quite, In a labyrinth of light—'). At the same time he illustrated Laurence Housman's story 'The Man in the Moon' for *The Pall Mall Magazine*, and here for the first time he successfully rose to a challenge; his illustrations 'reek of dread and ancient mystery', according to one critic. He joined the prestigious ranks of artists who contributed to the short-lived *The Butterfly* (1899–1900), contributing a Fuseli-inspired fantasy to illustrate 'The Incubus'. But *The Idler* lost money and eventually had to be sold in 1901. In fact by this time Sime was so embittered by his losses that he turned against all magazines: 'the worst possible form of publication – magazines! Those God-forsaken sponge-cakes of the suburban soul.' It is interesting to note, however, that Sime worked briefly for the American magazine publishing magnate William Randolph Hearst in 1905.

Sime turned instead to book illustration and fortunately teamed up with a valuable kindred spirit, the young, wealthy Irish nobleman fantasist Lord Dunsany. Together they were a match made in heaven, and they collaborated on the bizarre volumes of Dunsany's fantastical tales, like the quasi-oriental *The Gods of Pegana* (1905) and *Time and the Gods* (1906) followed by others in 1908, 1910, 1912 and 1916. It was indeed a sympathetic partnership, although on the surface it seemed ill-matched: while Sime was of humble origins and by then aged 40, Dunsany was of noble birth and just 26. By commissioning Sime to illustrate his first book

Fig. 9: Sidney Sime.

of tales, based upon a childhood love of the exotic (his mother was related to Sir Richard Burton, translator of *The Arabian Nights*, and he loved Hans Andersen's tales as well as stories from the Bible), Dunsany forged a long and valuable partnership and indeed friendship with Sime. Although he initially wanted Gustave Doré to illustrate his first volume, he turned to his second choice, Sime: 'This remarkable man consented to do me eight illustrations, and I have never seen a black-and-white artist with a more stupendous imagination.' Sime was rather cynical about the whole process; in time he felt his imagination prostituted by publishers and authors unable to imagine illustrations ('Only the sick need a physician'). 'But Dunsany's gods and never-never lands, boldly created in a language akin to that of the Authorized Version [of the Bible] would have chimed in with his own growing fascination with "other worlds than ours",' recalled his biographer. 'The texture of Dunsany's language and his kind of humour would have appealed to Sime; as would Dunsany's mastery of implication and suspense.' Like Sime, Dunsany was a troubled outsider, an avowed atheist who delighted in creating gods who like him were remote from the world and amused by human striving. He cursed his aristocratic heritage: 'The greatest barrier over which my dreams have had to climb appears to have been the belief that titled dilettantes trying to write, in order to take the bread out of the mouths of honest men, should be discouraged by every man of independent means.' It was to Dunsany's credit that he recognised Sime's genius (he had once written to a friend, 'Genius is in fact an infinite capacity for not taking pains'). 'So I left Mr Sime to do exactly what he liked.'[26]

It is interesting to note that Sime also admired the fantasist Arthur Machen, writer of tales mystical, romantic and macabre; he in fact provided frontispieces to Machen's *The House of Souls* (1906) and *The Hill of Dreams* (1907). Another kindred spirit, Machen wrote in *The Three Imposters* (a book which so terrified Conan Doyle he could not sleep after reading it), 'I yield to fantasy; I cannot withstand the influence of the grotesque.' However, there were limits to Sime's ambitions; when asked in 1911 to illustrate 'a costly and ornate volume of Edgar Allan Poe', Sime recoiled from the challenge: 'I am philandering with the project not feeling quite equal to my author. You see, I am looking forward to meeting Poe in Hell and I am loath to do anything that would embarrass the encounter.'[27]

Instead Sime continued to provide challenging illustrations to weekly papers like *The Illustrated London News*, *The Sketch*, *The Tatler* and *The Graphic*, where his quirky, rather mystifying fantasies appeared throughout the 1920s (cats 40–41). He created a series of twelve exotic fantasy creatures for 'The Sime Zoology: Beasts that might have been', which were republished in 1923 in one volume with jingles by Sime and musical scores by Josef Holbrooke as *The Bogey Beasts* (cat. 42).

He remained a true original to the end, a rare artistic outsider unmoved by the wave of modernism that swept through the 1920s. He was primarily a black and white illustrator, a disciple of Beardsley, but in later years he dabbled in oils and stage design. His influences were as diverse as his imagination: he shamelessly borrowed from the dense atmospheric prints of Piranesi and Meryon, the bold, spare power of Hokusai's woodcuts, and even his old friend and fellow renegade artist Augustus John. But Sime had depth. He was not a charmer, his talent was not superficial or just simply amusing; in fact, many felt his work was just too weird, too challenging or just plain confusing. In an age when publishers turned to photography and the more superficial demands of a fickle public, sadly Sime's inventions were not in demand. Book publishers wanted colour, and Sime could not compete with contemporaries like Edmund Dulac, Arthur Rackham, Kay Nielsen, Harry Clarke, the Detmold twins, Willy Pogany or the Robinsons, who willingly and successfully provided colour plates for the lucrative publisher's lavish gift book market. For consolation Sime turned inward to an eclectic world of his own making. He studied esoteric texts and spent long hours experimenting with electricity, with his telescope for star-gazing and even a microscope to investigate the bizarre elements of the insect world. He even studied chemistry and on one occasion he blew off the roof of his studio. Throughout this forced exile he continued to paint, adopting the eccentric habit of throwing matches on a table and painting the resulting pattern, usually working upon 20 or 30 canvases at one time. But despite all these

Fig. 10: Harry Clarke.

experiments, he died at Worplesdon, Surrey in 1941, a broken, forgotten fantasist: 'A genius whose stupendous imagination has passed across our time little more noticed by most people than the shadow of a bird passing over the lawn,' lamented his old friend and patron Lord Dunsany.

Harry Clarke

By the turn of the century, an element of internationalism began to creep into the Cult of Beardsley. Running parallel to the master's English career was his greatest exponent in Ireland, the 'most exotic of all the hot-house flowers', Harry Clarke (fig. 10). Clarke was in essence an Irish Symbolist, a representative of the Irish Celtic Revival who brought a unique talent for hard work and uncompromised fantasy into the many worlds in which he worked, including book illustration, stained glass designs for churches, painting and drawing and even costume design. His most recent biographer concurs he was 'the last of the Pre-Raphaelites… Ireland's only great Symbolist artist who virtually gave the Irish Renaissance its iconography in "a splendid afterglow" of unearthly and eccentric genius'. Others found him 'one of the strangest geniuses of his time… who might have incarnated here from the dark side of the moon.' Clarke's formula was not pure nostalgia, however: 'his art displays a wilful decadence and an ambivalent religious mysticism of medieval intensity which ranges from the sublimely beautiful to the grotesquely macabre, rarely found in the work of his Celtic peers'. There was in fact a similarity with Sime's fantastical world, particularly his Dunsany books, for Clarke echoed what 'in part is beautiful, part is complicated, part is unhealthy and the whole thing is unwholesome and intricate, especially in his Poe illustrations.'[28]

Born in Dublin on 17 March 1889, the son of a stained glass artist and decorator, he soon entered the family business, studying in the evenings at the Metropolitan School of Art under Sir William Orpen. He was awarded a travelling scholarship in 1913 and chose France, to study its medieval stained glass, being especially taken by the twelfth-century glass of Chartres. All the while he lived in Paris, soaking up the Parisian *fin de siècle* atmosphere – 'the poisonous honey of France'. There he found sympathetic writers and artists and fell under the spell of Huysmans and the Symbolist painter Gustave Moreau, whose works young Clarke adored, especially Moreau's version of *Salome*. Huysmans had once compared the sparkle of Moreau's colours to stained glass, and this also must have inspired the young Clarke when he attempted his own interpretations in glass. While in Paris, in 1914 the young Clarke befriended the Scottish fantasy designer Jessie King and her architect and stained glass designer husband E. A. Taylor, often visiting them at their Shealing Atelier. There, as well as listening to Taylor's outspoken views on stained glass design, he met ambitious new artists just like himself, and with his Irish sense of humour and gentle nature he charmed the guests. But even at this period, above all Clarke most admired Beardsley; like two kindred spirits these young artists shared literary and artistic tastes, and to the initiated they even shared physical appearances. There was one other significant parallel: both young artists had their careers cut tragically short by tuberculosis.

As an art student, Clarke was especially attracted to book illustration. He first worked in Beardsley's shadow, using the same sinewy black line, and in fact he completed a private commission of Beardsleyesque illustrations, his version of the favourite Beardsley subject, Pope's *Rape of the Lock*, in 1913 (cats 43–48). That same year he visited the London galleries, which he found filled with inspired original illustrations by Edmund Dulac and especially the Dane Kay Nielsen, whose *Powder and Crinoline* drawings were that year exhibited at the prestigious Leicester Galleries. He grew more catholic in his tastes and studied other works by his contemporaries: the drawings by Sidney Sime, Annie French, Jessie King and Alastair, and even the more exotic Russian stage designs of Leon Bakst (having seen Diaghilev's Ballets Russes in London in 1919) and the fellow Russian designer Erté. In fact, Clarke had made the frustrating rounds of London publishers in 1912, with his portfolio of black and white drawings rejected by most; he was taken up at the eleventh hour by George Harrap, the soon-to-be-doyen of the elaborately illustrated gift book, and patron to Dulac, Nielsen, Pogany and Rackham. Harrap had a good eye for new talent, and he knew his market. He immediately pronounced

Clarke 'this Irish genius', knowing even his early illustrations were unique to the period. Eventually the publisher's lavish productions of Clarke's illustrations, printed in colour as well as black and white, sold hugely well, some titles going into four editions and then being reprinted. These included editions of *Hans Andersen's Fairy Tales* (1916), of Edgar Allan Poe's *Tales of Mystery and Imagination* (1919), a series of tales under the title *The Years at the Spring* (1920), *Fairy Tales of Perrault* (1922), Goethe's *Faust* (1925) and *Selected Poems of Swinburne* (1928).

Like Beardsley, Clarke had an inherent skill with pen and ink line, matching it with blocks of solid black to create startling compositions which even today remain memorable. According to his biographer, his was 'an unswerving tendency towards the fantastic which was also reminiscent of Beardsley, and his powers of imagination had full play in the psychic interpretation of the weird and macabre literature he was called to illustrate.' His Poe illustrations were among the most successfully horrific ever to interpret the pages of that author's works. His professional career began with sixteen full-page watercolour and 24 decorative black and white drawings for Hans Andersen's *Fairy Tales*, which Harrap declared 'of the character that is usually entrusted only to artists who have "arrived".' Clarke was at first very reticent to do colour work, but Harrap recalled how he insisted: 'I said to him… that his pen and ink work teemed so greatly with colour that there could be no question as to his ability to provide the colour illustrations people so much enjoy'. His work schedule was strict, a daily routine from 10.30am to 7pm seven days a week, working in pairs to avoid staleness; it took a week for a colour drawing, just four days for black and white. But in the end, the Andersen drawings made his reputation. When published in 1916, issued in both ordinary and special signed limited editions bound in vellum, they competed favourably with the highly successful Edmund Dulac version of *Hans Andersen's Tales* published by Hodder and Stoughton in 1911, as well as Nielsen's fanciful *In Powder and Crinoline*, published in 1912. In fact, these were the artists who were to become his rivals as well as his inspiration; Harrap soon cherished Clarke as his lucrative new star, the publisher's answer in combating the gift book competition provided by Nielsen, Dulac and especially Arthur Rackham.

Clarke moved on to Poe's *Tales of Mystery and Imagination*, which was published in 1919 (cat. 49). Many consider this work to be his masterpiece. Even the critics agreed his 24 full-page and twelve small macabre black and white drawings were especially suited to Poe's horrific genius: 'Never before, I think, have these marvellous tales been visually interpreted with such flesh-creeping, brain-haunting illusions of horror, terror and the unspeakable,' waxed the *Studio* critic, while the *Irish Times* called them 'wild imaginings with which the unbridled fancy could play, dark and jewelled magnificence, terror and wonder – all cast in a tone of a delicate and gloomy beauty'.[29] Harrap was so pleased with the concept that in late autumn 1919 he issued Clarke's illustrations in four separate editions (bound in cloth, velvet, full morocco leather, and a vellum deluxe edition of just 170 copies on handmade paper). He even gave it lavish publicity for the Christmas market, and sales proved 'hugely successful': the book went into a new edition by 1923, and a third printing by 1928. For this Clarke was paid 100 guineas for his drawings, but it was his critical success which was more valuable to him at the time: *The Irish Statesman* concluded how 'horror and intense feeling are depicted with a grace and beauty of detail that lift the designs far above morbidity… the artist has cast them [the settings] into a bizarre world of his own fashioning, where strange plants flourish and the people are clad in costumes of unexperienced richness and beauty.'[30]

Clarke had an endearing, wide-eyed, kind and generous nature; a charming conversationalist, he was witty, observant and incisive. His subtle sense of humour filled most of his works with a distinctive air of the fantastic, and yet he was hard working and devoted himself not only to his illustrations but also the stained glass business he had inherited from his father. Many of the concepts he perfected on paper found their way into his glass designs, drawn to shimmer against jewel-like colour in emulation of his beloved medieval masters, though his figures were unmistakably his own. By 1918, the Clarke world of the fantastic was peopled by the strangest characters as he masked their ears, necks and wrists, or covered them in mock medieval style with exotic helmets, or dressed them in large collars and high ruched necklines, tapering cuffs and sleeves. He loved to stylise his figures, standing them upon tapering toes or even cloven hooves, and giving them elongated fingers, as seen in one of his last drawings, the 'Falstaffian figure' exhibited here (cat. 51). When asked why he took such inventive liberties with his figures, he shrugged, 'That's my gadget,' or 'Because I like it,' and yet he remained touchingly humble despite his success as an illustrator: 'I feel I do not do a book as it should be done. I see my drawings and there is only a hazy background of Book, whereas the drawings should, as you have so many times said, be subordinate to the whole – or an item in a complete scheme'.[31] He soon gave up illustration and succumbed to the pressures of running the family glass factory in Dublin. There he and his assistants created numerous liturgical designs for church windows throughout Ireland, one in England (the chapel at Ashdown Park, Sussex) and even America. In time he was considered a master fantasist in glass, and he perfected the jewelled plate glass technique which he etched or drew with his own distinctive wide-eyed figures and Celtic designs. His reputation grew but, tempered by painful attacks of tuberculosis, his health gradually failed. Harry Clarke, the Irish wizard, died tragically young, aged just 41, at a Davos clinic in 1931.

THE AGE OF COLOUR

*I*N THE EARLY TWENTIETH CENTURY artistic tastes were changing. People wanted colour, escapism and the infectious delights of the exotic, particularly to help them forget the terrible horrors of the First World War. Indeed, enterprising wartime publishers had produced elaborate colour illustrated volumes to be sold on behalf of the war effort, with the finest artist-illustrators like Arthur Rackham and Edmund Dulac willingly contributing some of their best and most powerfully stirring illustrations to aid the cause. Edwardian frivolity now took on a new seriousness, which many saw as a longing for a return to a lost world of pre-war innocence. Soldiers in the battlefield, forced to decamp from their home cities, towns and villages, clutched mementos of their idyllic homeland: books of poetry, picture postcards of the churches, fields and villages that made Britain great. 'This is what you are fighting for,' they seemed to say, and it was a sentiment which continued to motivate a post-war Britain as well.

Others turned to the Empire, especially to the appeal of India and the Far East. It is not surprising that the archetypal Edwardian novelist E. M. Forster openly professed that he 'loved all things exotic'. The Empire could provide the illusion of escape, especially through the stories of Rudyard Kipling's India, which appealed to a huge audience. Although many illustrators and even so-called fine art painters, especially society portraitists like William Nicholson, had lost valuable commissions during the war period (their patrons considering it unpatriotic to spend money on art when the country was in danger), publishers recognised and capitalised on the change in their market. They beefed up their production skills and offered books of lavish colour plates, like the elaborately produced editions of Kipling's *Jungle Books* illustrated by the Detmolds. The highly lucrative children's market also grew: William Nicholson's children's classic, *The Un-Common Cat* (1895), went into numerous editions by the turn of the century, and copies were dismembered for framing to decorate the nurseries of the Empire well into the twentieth century; a second more lavish edition was then sold to the nation's doting parents, or what *The Art Journal* called 'children of a larger growth'.

With the success of the colour illustrated gift book, it soon became clear that colour was beginning to play an increasingly important role in book publishing. Those dull Victorian volumes of dense black and white wood engravings gave way to the three-colour printing process which soon revolutionised the illustrated book market. This ingenious technical process was derived from the half-tone printing of black and white images which had been perfected as long ago as 1882 by Georg Meisenbach, but only put into general use for colour work from 1904–05. Artists rose to the challenge and, knowing their original drawings could now be saved and profitably sold after reproduction, they learned to paint in the clear, even-toned watercolour washes which were printed as separate plates onto a fine, shiny paper. These plates were often 'tipped' or pasted into a book upon rough paper backgrounds, surrounded by elaborate borders and protected from grimy fingers by tissue guards. This certainly lent an air of preciosity to each volume of what was once a commonplace publication. Jessie King learned these necessary skills, as did her colleagues and rivals Harry Clarke, Charles Robinson, Edmund Dulac, Willy Pogany and of course the supreme master of the gift book, Arthur Rackham.

Moreover, tastes in popular entertainment changed too. *The New Statesmen* in 1914 lamented how fewer books were taken out of the public libraries owing to the popularity of that more immediately gratifying pastime, the cinema, or, as it was known then, the 'flicks'. Indeed the local urban cinema soon took the brunt of the blame for not only the decline in literacy but also the rise in bad behaviour among the young, with gangs of impressionable teenage youths terrorising the locals of Manchester and Glasgow in imitation of the tribes of irate Red Indians they had seen on the big screen. In 1911, a series of school strikes also occurred, with children emulating the striking elders they had seen in the cinema newsreels. In addition, the theatre grew more appealing to a larger audience with more exotically-themed plays, sets and costumes, like Charles Ricketts's South American fantasies, or the colourful creations of the Ballets Russes which took London by storm in 1919. To accompany these productions the London streets were filled with eye-catching posters often designed by theatre's most talented new designers. As the *New Republic* predicted so astutely in 1894, in an article titled 'The Art of Hoarding', a new populist aesthetic would be born on the streets: 'London will soon be resplendent with advertisements, and against a leaden sky skysigns will trace their formal arabesque. Beauty has laid siege to the city, and the telegraph wires shall no longer be the sole joy of our aesthetic perceptions.'[32] In fact many of the period's most popular artists of the illustrated book, like Ricketts, Dulac and Nielsen, also tried their hand at theatrical designs. Moreover Arthur Rackham was rumoured to have been invited (but declined) an invitation by Walt Disney to work on his fantasy films, while his illustrator colleagues Pogany and Nielsen succumbed to the Hollywood challenge. In time the gap between popular and High Art would be blurred even further as the cinema, the art gallery and the theatre vied for greater popularity among the burgeoning new generations of the Modern Age.

'I BELIEVE IN FAIRIES'

FOR MANY CHILDREN AS WELL AS ADULTS, fantasy meant fairies. Their ethereal world at the bottom of the garden provided a rich and satisfying means of escapism. It was the age of *Peter Pan*, with the first stage production of J. M. Barrie's famous story designed by the painter William Nicholson in 1904. The audience of adults as well as children who were enthralled by Barrie's story was ripe for other flights of fancy as well. 'I remember I used to half believe and wholly play with fairies when I was a child,' recalled a mature Beatrix Potter. She confided in her journal how the archetypal images of fairies and fairyland greatly inspired artists of her generation: 'I cannot tell what possesses me with the fancy that they laugh and clap their hands, especially the little ones that grow in troops and rings amongst dead leaves in the woods. I suppose it is the fairy rings, the myriads of fairy fungi that start into life in autumn woods.' For Potter, the legendary loner devoted wholly to her vision of nature, such sights and impressions were paramount to her childhood and indeed later to her artistic career: 'What heaven can be more real than to retain the spirit-world of childhood, tempered and balanced by knowledge and common-sense, to fear no longer the terror that flieth by night, yet to feel truly and understand a little, a very little, of the story of life.'[33] The Victorians perfected the world of fairyland: their masters – like the artist-illustrator Richard Doyle, the reclusive painter of tortured fantasies John Anster Fitzgerald, and the mentally unstable painter Richard Dadd – provided the visual vocabulary which would influence generations of artists and especially children's illustrators long after the Victorians. It was public knowledge that even Queen Victoria loved fairyland. Her favourite legend involved the fate of Undine, the watersprite, whose portrait she once purchased for her beloved Albert; moreover Disraeli nicknamed Her Majesty 'The Faery' in reference to Spenser's *Faerie Queene*.

One of the most extraordinary exponents of fairyland was the Arts and Crafts woodcut artist Bernard Sleigh (1872–1954). As an established and competent artist-engraver, he had wood engraved illustrations for *The Dome* and *The Yellow Book*, and also engraved at least one design by Charles Ricketts, as well as engraving the Arts and Crafts illustrator Arthur Gaskin's illustrations to Hans Andersen. Then he became mesmerised by fairies, and the discovery transformed his life and his career. His delightful large chiaroscuro woodcut, 'The Horns of Elfland Faintly Blowing' is typical of this new-found obsession with fairyland (cat. 52). Sleigh was in fact a curious psychological case, who proudly proclaimed in the preface to his own publication *A Faery Calendar*, 'I believe in Faeries. It is very natural and not a bit foolish; for in these days we are quickly learning how little we know of any other world than our own.' Moreover, he aptly called his autobiography *Memoirs of a Human Peter Pan*. He worked hard to propagate his message and instil his fascination with the ethereal in three volumes: *Ancient Mappe of Fairyland* (1918), *A Faerie Calendar* (1920) and *A Faerie Pageant* (1924). In each illustration he developed a distinctive style, using a bold line, and with castles and landscapes he introduced an air of heavy medievalism which interjected a stronger, less fey note to the fairy canon. It is not surprising that Sleigh's work is contemporary with another landmark work in the fairy world, the so-called Cottingley fairy mystery – the hoaxed photographs taken of fairies by Elsie Wright and Frances Griffiths in between 1917 and 1920 – and the fairy researches of their champion Sir Arthur Conan Doyle (nephew to the fairy painter Richard Doyle), who published his own proselytising volume, *The Coming of the Fairies*, in 1922. Fairyland subjects would maintain a foothold in the publications and decorative arts of Britain throughout the twentieth century and indeed into the twenty-first.

THE GLASGOW SCHOOL

Jessie Marion King

*I*T WAS THIS WHIMSICAL, not to say more joyful world, which inspired the extraordinarily prolific Scottish artist Jessie Marion King (fig. 11). 'It is to the bank of fancy we must go to find Miss King,' her devoted husband, the artist and critic Ernest Archibald Taylor, enthused, 'where the pebbles dot over the shore, and the butterfly shells whisper of the sea beyond, and the sand-dune roses tell of the joys of the surf-wind; deep down, too, as they twine through the crumbling loam, and as you listen and wend your way over the heather-padded slopes to the woods of chattering leaves, and hear a feather-tuft sing.' Indeed, this was a far cry from Beardsley's satanic world, although Jessie King, as a young Glasgow Art School student, much admired and was influenced by Beardsley's technical prowess with pen and ink. 'But the critic who sees in the work of Miss King the same personalities as in Beardsley is only a superficial observer,' Taylor concluded. 'It is like calling a harebell a forget-me-not.' The light, ethereal world of Miss King was enchanting, some would say slight and poorly conceived ('A well-known critic told me one day Miss King's work was only a trick, but she could do it,' Taylor recalled).[34] But Jessie King's illustrations touched a chord, and her choice of Arthurian legends and Scottish folk ballads or even favourite nursery tales (her most cherished was 'The Forsaken Merman') helped her to create a distinctive and influential canon of endearing book illustrations which remain popular today. Moreover, her talents, honed on the Glasgow School tenets of Arts and Crafts and fine decorative design, were successfully turned to mural painting, ceramics, bookbinding, jewellery design, embroidery, and dress and fabric design. (The vogue in batik printing was fuelled by her how-to book based upon the fairy tale 'Cinderella'.) She even designed an entire children's nursery complete with doll's house and toys (fig. 12, cat. 61).

Such a multi-faceted talent surprisingly grew out of a dour, severely restrictive childhood. Born in 1875, the daughter of a strict clergyman father who was intent upon a 'no nonsense education', young Jessie took to hiding her sketches in the hedges before returning home from school for fear they would be torn up by her compliant mother. At the Glasgow School of Art from 1892, she fell under the spell of the so-called Glasgow Style, perfected by 'The Spooks', the four talented students Frances and Margaret Macdonald, Herbert MacNair and Charles Rennie Mackintosh, who brought an air of elevated purity and seriousness to a curriculum previously hidebound to fine art aspirations. Here crafts and handiwork prepared the students for a life in commerce, safely armed with the necessary skills which could be adapted in the burgeoning pre-war decorative arts marketplace. But King had a romantic nature: she loved the exotic, and when her first work was published in the prestigious *The Studio* in 1898, it was called 'The Light of Asia', 'drawn with a knowledge of form and refinement of line that disarm criticism and command admiration', waxed the magazine's critic. Indeed her work appeared frequently in *The Studio* for over twelve years and in 1902 she was even the subject of an elaborate illustrated survey much like the one that had launched young Beardsley in 1893. This was also the year she exhibited with her art school colleagues at the prestigious Turin Exhibition of Decorative Art, where she was awarded a gold medal for a book cover design.

Then followed two prestigious book illustration commissions: 23 full-page illustrations in black and red for an edition of *The High History of*

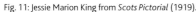

Fig. 11: Jessie Marion King from *Scots Pictorial* (1919).

Fig. 12: Jessie King-designed nursery, 1913 (see cat. 61).

the Holy Graal (1903), published by J. M. Dent in both standard and deluxe vellum-bound editions, and *The Defence of Guenevere and Other Poems* by William Morris (1904), for John Lane at the Bodley Head (cats 59–60). Significantly, it was this second commission by Beardsley's first publisher which gave her the greatest inspiration; she created 95 line drawings for it, 22 full-page, and designed the red cloth binding for the book which, more than any other, contributed to her reputation as an illustrator. She continued to explore the illustrated book, from 1901 to 1931 designing innovative book wrappers for upmarket paperbacks which were printed in colour on semi-translucent papers by the Glasgow firm of Gowans and Gray. Titles varied from *Everyman* and the plays of Maurice Maeterlinck, to little nature books like *Our Trees and How to Know Them* and whimsical books for children such as *Why the Fuchsia Hangs His Head*. She also wrote and illustrated her own stories. As a topographer she produced volumes of views of favourite sites in Glasgow, Edinburgh and later Kirkcudbright, the most successful, however, being *The Book of Bridges*, which captured her love of Parisian streets.

Poetry was a great love and she turned to pocket-sized editions of popular collections, like *The Flowers of Parnassus* for John Lane, or the 'Golden Poets' series and Broadway Booklets for George Routledge, in which she interpreted the poems of Milton, Spenser, Keats and Tennyson. These suggested a shift in style, brought on by her move to Paris. King had married her fellow art student Ernest Archibald Taylor, and they worked well together, moving in 1911–15 to Paris to run The Shealing Atelier of Oil and Watercolour Painting, Design and the Applied Arts. There they established an artistic centre where eager young artists from Britain descended, like the young Harry Clarke, who would present copies of his newest books to the couple he had found so charming and welcoming in his student days. Indeed, they took young Harry under their wing and bolstered his confidence enough to pursue his chosen artistic career. Here too, King discovered the Ballets Russes and the vibrant colours and fiery energy of Leon Bakst's designs, and she was transfixed. Her own colours turned intense, one critic called them 'piercing, unexpected colour eccentricities' and she now experimented with highly coloured inks and a greater fluidity in her drawings, especially in her illustrated edition of Oscar Wilde's *A House of Pomegranates* (1915). Here also, for the first time, appeared a new exoticism; yet among the several terse, sinuous, oriental-looking colour plates were other more traditional landscapes which recall her love of the blue mountain peaks of her beloved Arran hills (cats 57–58).

An endearing character, Jessie King loved to dress up; she wore wide floppy hats and the mock medieval dresses she once designed for various pageants. With her love of nature and plants in particular, she could often be found sketching in the open air, dressed in a long black cape, silver buckled shoes and wide hat, or seen freewheeling her bicycle down the hills and throughout her favourite Scottish villages. Children loved her; as one recalled, 'Jessie always made you feel important – made you feel she was on your side.' She drew for them, mended their toys, told them stories and, since much of her work was firmly grounded in their infantile world, she was a great favourite. Even her larger finished watercolours had such beguiling titles as 'The Cricket', 'The House with the Evil Eyes', 'Yon Far Isle Beyond the Enchanted Sea', 'The Spell of the Moon', 'All the Day's Filled with Sunshine' and 'Sing Out for the Happy You Feel Inside'. Her acknowledged influences were particular and quite intriguing: certainly Beardsley, whom she loved as a student; the Pre-Raphaelites, whom she also learned to emulate at art school; Japanese prints; Botticelli, surprisingly; as well as the works by her friends and contemporaries Harry Clarke, Sidney Sime and Willy Pogany – a posthumous inventory of her library revealed volumes by all of these artists.

As a decorative artist, Jessie King's designs succeeded well into the Modern Age. While book commissions dried up in post-war years, she gave batik classes and pioneered the fashionable fabric printing technique, designing clothing and selling scarves to Liberty's in London. As a jewellery designer, she excelled. Like her fellow Glasgow Art School colleagues, she had prepared designs to submit to Liberty's in London, and those accepted were machine-produced in Birmingham, the more intricate stone setting and burnishing done by hand. Liberty's had pioneered the field of handcrafted silver, from 1899 issuing a series of Celtic designs which set the stage for many future successful lines, many of which originated with the Glasgow School designers. King's work was issued largely anonymously, but there is a purity and an understanding of the materials which mark her designs out from the more mundane. Similarly, she produced decorated under-glazed pottery, using favourite fairy tales and legends as her themes, and painting these designs directly upon the biscuitware surfaces. It was an artistic process she found quite challenging; in time the popularity of her nearly mass-produced pottery grew and it went on sale locally at the Paul Jones café-cum-craft shop in Kirkcudbright.

Unusually for an artist, Jessie King was a competent businesswoman, both highly organised and efficient – there is a delightful tale of her packing only one case for a visit to Paris, while her husband filled twelve. She worked constantly and exhibited in Glasgow and Edinburgh right up to her death on 3 August 1949. A legendary figure, with a fairy godmother-like appearance in wide-brimmed hat and long cloak, she exuded a distinctive charm. Always claiming a gift of second sight, and suffering from myopia, hers was the vision of a true miniaturist and she was able to create the gossamer-like surfaces of silver ink on vellum, as in 'The White Lady' (cat. 55), and later the highly charged watercolour jewels on vellum, like 'The Sea Voices', which remain her legacy today (cat. 57). In addition, her seemingly countless designs for the decorative arts, jewellery, fabrics and ceramics sit well alongside the over 200 illustration commissions she created in her long and productive lifetime.

Annie French

The gossamer mantle of Jessie King fell to her colleague at the Glasgow School of Art, Annie French. This talented decorative watercolourist was noted for her equally distinctive style, which was once characterised by an admirer as a 'lace-maker' who created figures, mostly of women in billowy dresses or 'spirits composed of cobwebs rather than creatures of flesh and blood'. In 1909 Annie French in fact succeeded Jessie King in the Design Department of the Glasgow School of Art, where she remained until 1914, when she married the artist George Wooliscroft Rhead and settled in London. In their early days, however, their paths crossed in their native city.

Born in Glasgow in 1872, the daughter of a metallurgist, Annie French studied from 1896 to 1902 under the legendary Francis Newbery at the Glasgow School of Art, as well as with the Belgian Symbolist painter Jean Delville who taught at the school from 1898 to 1902. She quickly devised her own highly decorative style, usually painting in fine stipple colour using an almost 'confetti-like texture' upon brown prepared paper or board, but most often on vellum, not unlike a medieval manuscript illuminator. Her influences were those early jewel-like surfaces of the Pre-Raphaelite illustrators, the sinewy line of Beardsley and of course Jessie King herself. This she turned most successfully to greetings card and postcard designs, as well as to the pointillist watercolours she showed regularly at the Royal Glasgow Institute from 1904, the RA in London from 1909 until the 1920s, and also in Liverpool, Paris and Canada. She died in Jersey in 1965, outliving her mentor by sixteen years.

There was a spiritual affinity between the two Glasgow women, their subjects chosen with the same air of whimsicality and love of the ethereal. In fact Annie French's titles for works could easily have been those used by Jessie King: 'The Floral Dress', 'The Lace Train', 'Fairies' Invitation', 'The Unhappy Prince', 'The Plumed Hat'. But Annie French imbued her surfaces with a mystical haze, created by thousands of tiny brush dots, which, like the photoengraved reproductions of the period with their screened images, lent a mystery to rather ordinary subjects. And, of course, there were the dresses, those billowy gowns which pay homage to the late neo-rococo pointillist drawings of their supreme master Aubrey Beardsley (cats 62–64).

MASTER ENCHANTERS

Arthur Rackham, RI

ARTHUR RACKHAM WAS ONE OF the most successful and influential colour book illustrators of the early twentieth century (fig. 13). Even today he is justly lauded for his remarkable influence upon the burgeoning colour gift book market.[35] His career spanned nearly 40 years and in that time he created about 150 illustrated books, published 3,000 illustrations, as well as painting numerous works in oil and watercolour for the galleries alone. His popularity was international, especially upon the continent and in America, where his books have never been out of print. The Rackham style, with its grotesque trees and ghoulish creatures, the fairy tales of sylvan glades and classical maidens, his pictured worlds of Shakespeare, Hans Andersen, the Grimm Brothers and Lewis Carroll, have charmed, terrified and delighted generations of adults and children alike.

Born in 1867, the son of a London legal secretary, young Arthur

Fig. 13: Arthur Rackham.

Rackham studied, drew and painted his surroundings, journeyed to Australia, and came back intent upon a career as an artist. While a clerk in the Westminster Fire Office, for eight years he attended evening classes at the influential Lambeth School of Art, where he met future illustration colleagues Laurence Housman, Charles Ricketts ('an inspiring influence and classmate') and Ricketts's future partner, the painter Charles Shannon ('a little god'). There he developed his drawing skills for a future in commercial illustration. Indeed he secured several early black and white drawing commissions for popular magazines, drawing the Prime Minister and Thomas Carlyle's Chelsea house for the *Westminster Gazette* and *Pall Mall Budget*, and quickly learned to turn his deft pen and ink sketches into other marketable subjects. However, knowing he wanted to become a painter and exhibit in the prestigious London galleries, he began to paint landscape watercolours which he successfully exhibited at the Royal Academy and Royal Watercolour Society.

Such work was not lucrative, however, so young Arthur returned to illustration and was commissioned by J. M. Dent to illustrate a new edition of *The Ingoldsby Legends*, his 80 black and white drawings and twelve colour plates appearing in 1898. His fellow Dent artist at the time was Aubrey Beardsley, whose approach to a common favoured medievalism (and recently published book *Le Morte Darthur*) greatly inspired Rackham. He would always be an historicist, locked in the past, where he found inspiration, especially in the Germanic – the Dürer woodcuts, the fantasies of Bosch, Grünewald and Altdorfer – but he also kept a collection of the more grotesque psychotic caricatures of the Frenchman Honoré Daumier, which inspired his own fantastical characterisations. Other Dent commissions followed, including illustrated editions of his favourite *Grimm's Fairy Tales*, and *Gulliver's Travels* in 1900. But it was with his 51 drawings to *Rip Van Winkle*, published in 1904, that Rackham finally achieved serious recognition.

Colour was a real challenge for Rackham. He insisted upon subtlety at all costs, sought inspiration in the delicate and the subdued. He loved the musty solemnity of medieval manuscripts, the pale yellows of aging paper and dusty faded colours. His 50 colour plates to J. M. Barrie's *Peter Pan*, which appeared in 1906, were an homage to this colour sense as well as to his Victorian forebears, which he spiced up with his own particular brand of strong linear grotesque fantasy. The book sold very well (14,000 copies of the six-shilling edition alone) and was eventually translated into several languages – including French, which inspired Claude Debussy to compose a piece based upon one of the illustrations for his daughter. By now Rackham was in his late thirties, and, with his own family to support, he was characteristically cautious of his successes. Always humble and self-effacing, he claimed his large workload was 'a question of nervous output' and never calculated, although his jealous rivals like Edmund Dulac continued to haunt his successes. In fact such was his fear of Dulac threatening his lucrative marketplace that Rackham ordered his publishers to send him all reviews and cuttings about Dulac's books so that he might prepare himself for any new rivalry.

The Rackham book reigned supreme for a time, buoyed up by good reviews and his publishers' respect for and determination to reproduce his delicate, parchment watercolours as best they could. Bound in gold-blocked leather or cloth of his own design, with endpapers printed from his drawings and colour plates 'tipped' in separately onto heavier paper, the Rackham gift book set the trend among publishers. Each beautifully presented volume was issued, for maximum sales, in a cheaper trade edition as well as a limited signed and numbered deluxe edition intended for the adult collector. Usually published three months before Christmas, and accompanied by an exhibition and sale of the original drawings at the London Leicester Galleries, the Rackham formula sold in its thousands. Some readily dismissed these as 'bound up portfolios of pictures', but to Rackham they were labours of love. In fact he became expert at overseeing the reproductions, haranguing his printers for minute changes as 'these initial matters need such careful attention – or the damage is done beyond recall'. It was apparent to all who worked with him that he was a perfectionist; it was a matter of principle to present his drawings as well printed as technically possible, and throughout his career Rackham was always, despite imitators and rivals, intent upon creating the best work he could for his adoring public.[36]

Never a modernist, or a sympathiser with the ephemeral nature of the fast-paced modern world, he abhorred its influences and inventions, like photography (which eventually threatened his career), the telephone, the motor car and even the typewriter and wristwatch. He remained all his life embedded in the past, revelling in the ancient stories, folk tales and fairy tales which he collected and told with great skill. Some found his visions too horrible for children, but Rackham insisted that 'the modern child is proof against the childish fears of former times'. His nephew recalled a visit to Kensington Gardens while Rackham was at work upon *Peter Pan*: 'He would make one gaze fixedly at one of the majestic trees with massive trunk and tell me about Grimm's fairy-tales, which he had illustrated, and about the little men who blew their horns in elfland. He would say that under the roots of that tree the little men had their dinner and churned the butter they extracted from the sap of the tree. He would also make me see queer animals and birds in the branches of the tree and a little magic door below the trunk, which was the entrance to Fairyland.'[37]

Fantasy was his strongest language, and classic fairy tales provided the perfect inspiration. An illustrated volume of *Aesop's Fables* in 1912 was followed by *Mother Goose* in 1913, and with these two works his children's market was secured. But as he had seen his reputation challenged by rivals, he had felt the need to develop more sophisticated adult themes, and with his love of the Germanic he turned to his beloved Wagner, and illustrated volumes of *The Rhinegold and the Valkyrie* in 1910 (cat. 67), followed by *Siegfried and the Twilight of the Gods* in 1911. These confused his public and were not great successes, but he persevered with the adult themes. More successfully he had turned to Shakespeare, and created what is generally considered to be his masterpiece, *A Midsummer Night's Dream*, which was completed in 1908. This became one of the most influential illustrated books of the early twentieth century, inspiring ballets and stage designs. Rackham's ethereal world of sylvan landscapes enhanced the timelessness of Shakespeare's tale, and he chose each sequence to illustrate himself and eventually produced two separate book editions of the play.

In addition, Rackham's sea fantasies are unforgettable. He could call up the sea's enchanting folklore in a single watercolour, like 'The Widow Whitgift' exhibited here (cat. 65). Borrowing from the Victorian love of sea legends, he delighted in marine characters, especially female ones, like the tale of the watersprite, Undine, which was one of Queen Victoria's favourites. Undine was the beautiful water nymph who had no soul until she married a human. Rackham transformed the spirit of these legends into his own watery, murky Gothic world, and his illustrated version of *Undine* appeared in 1909. However, even in his more adult Wagnerian illustrations he was inspired by the sea, especially those horrific scenes of howling sirens – the harpies of classical times – whose screaming, flailing bodies and sinewy hair he drew in perfect homage to the period's Art Nouveau design sensibilities so beloved and explored by the French sculptors Raoul Larche and Emile Gregoire (cats 68–69). Moreover, it was his mastery of atmosphere and ability to create a terrifying Gothic vision which greatly struck the young impressionable C. S. Lewis, who felt 'the sky had turned round' when he first saw Rackham's Wagnerian illustrations: 'Pure Northernness engulfed me: a vision of large, clear spaces hanging above the Atlantic in the endless twilight of a Northern summer'.[38]

Rackham's career began to wane and he turned inwards, eschewing the commercial world to paint for his own pleasure and for the galleries. Some works incorporated favourite fairy tale subjects or much-loved poetry. He had long admired the now classic *Goblin Market* poem by Christina Rossetti, which Housman had so expertly interpreted years earlier, and created his own coloured version (cat. 66). Other paintings he created for sheer pleasure – pure landscapes taken from his rural surroundings in Sussex. His nephew recalled how completely his uncle shut himself away from the horrors of the world, tucked in his studio, 'the only truly happy man I have come across because he was absorbed in his work to the exclusion of everything else, and even the grim war news and the air raids left him untroubled'.[39] After the war, despite a resurgence in commissions, books with Rackham designs were poorly printed on cheaper paper, wartime economies having taken their toll. 'The freely illustrated Rackham book is no longer possible,' he lamented. Most notable of these later volumes was his homage to Aubrey Beardsley: 28 black and white and twelve colour illustrations to Edgar Allan Poe's *Tales of Mystery and Imagination* (1935). This proved quite a struggle to produce: Rackham told a young admirer while he was drawing the stories his inventions, 'were so horrible I was beginning to frighten myself'. His final volume, over which he lavished characteristic care despite bouts of severe pain from a life-threatening cancer, was Kenneth Grahame's *Wind in the Willows*, which was issued posthumously in 1940. Rackham died on 6 September 1939, just three days after Britain declared war on Germany; his friends believed it was a blessed release for such a gentle soul, for Rackham felt he could never face yet another disastrous war.

Charles Robinson, RI

Almost exactly contemporary with Arthur Rackham's career was that of the beloved children's illustrator Charles Robinson. Indeed the two artists shared much in the way of temperament, especially their mutual love of the folk and fairy tales they both illustrated, including works by Wagner, which helped them secure a large and enthusiastic public. Robinson was born in London on 22 October 1870, into a large family of printer-craftsmen (his grandfather was a wood engraver, his father an illustrator). Among his four brothers were Thomas and William Heath, both destined to become famous for their own brands of competent black and white and whimsical illustrations. Although his brothers received proper full-time art school educations, due to financial constraints young Charles had to make do with only evening classes, which he regretted, although William thought this lack of formal training was a definite advantage in maintaining the distinctive childlike approach young Charles perfected so well throughout his career; the regime of long hours copying casts 'would have checked his delightful freedom and his most original fancy'.[40]

Early published drawings were merely imitative of Aubrey Beardsley, whose influence often rankled as Charles tried to find his own style while completing endless piles of hack work for the illustrated magazine market. He even created a small booklet of Christmas card designs parodying Beardsley as 'Christmas Dreams by Awfly Weirdly'. In 1895, *The Studio*, that powerful barometer of current artistic taste, found Robinson had the talent to be more than his obvious mentors, Beardsley, Ricketts and Anning Bell, for with Charles 'one may expect a personal style that will take a far higher place'.[41] In fact this was the year Robinson published illustrations to his first and most important commission, Robert Louis Stevenson's *A Child's Garden of Verses*. Published by that entrepreneur of the precious collectors' editions, John Lane, in a very limited edition of 150 copies, it was so popular it was reprinted many times until 1952; as the *New York Bookman* perceptively noted, Robinson 'has depicted childhood in all its remoteness from the grown-up land, in its heroic and fantastic imaginings, in its long thoughts and its short sight'.[42] With this one book, Robinson had joined the prestigious ranks of the Lane band of artist-authors, which included not only Walter Crane, whom Charles greatly admired and emulated, as well as Aubrey Beardsley, but also the literary pantheon of writers like Henry James and Edmund Gosse.

Robinson became largely known for his children's themes and illustrated over a hundred volumes in black and white and pale, delicate watercolour. 'The Spotted Mimulus' is a prime example of his sure pen and ink work (cat. 70). He loved children and eventually had six of his own, whom he willingly pressed into modelling for him. They gave him his trademark style; according to his biographer, 'the fearless Charles Robinson child, with his thick wavy hair and rustic clothes, encountered by many for the first time gambolling his way through Stevenson's poems, is to be found somewhere… and just as Arthur Rackham became inseparable from his wizened elves and dwarfs, so the public expected of Charles Robinson his graphic evocation of childhood played out by the innocent, and not so innocent, characters who ran riot or just dallied, across the "Land of Counterpane" and "Up the Mountainside of Dreams"'. On the other hand he was not always appreciated by children, as one wealthy Edwardian recalled of her parents moving to a 30-bedroomed house in Oxfordshire where her nursery shelves groaned under the weight of Robinson titles: 'The nursery was full of his books for which I suppose that the grown-ups saw in him graces hidden from the young. From our point of view he had several bad vices, such as wasting the paper by filling it up with meaningless swirls and smoking candles and being able to draw only two children, a curly-haired one and a straight-haired one.'[43]

Fig. 14: Robinson's cover design for *The Sensitive Plant* (1911).

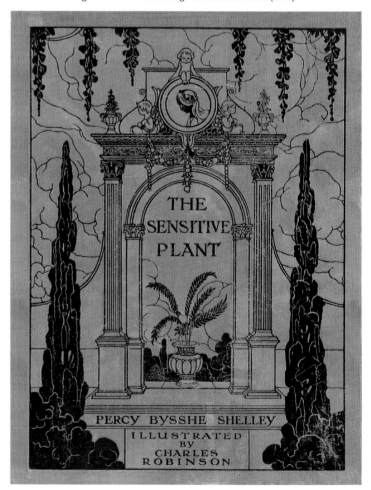

In time there were other, more sophisticated subjects, bound in elaborate gilt and red cloth designs of his own invention, like his version of Anatole France's delightful *Bee* (cat. 73). There were also lavish watercolour plates of long-gowned women or adoring mothers languishing in floral gardens for a version of Shelley's *The Sensitive Plant*, in 1911 (fig. 14 cat. 72). He also mixed a heady exoticism in the colour plates to an edition of Oscar Wilde's *The Happy Prince* (1913). However, he returned relentlessly to his proven market and retained a naïve innocence in the drawings for his numerous and very popular collections of fairy tales. Indeed it soon became clear Robinson was first and foremost a decorative artist who believed in the total design of the book. Like Rackham, he was talented enough to borrow from the past, from the townscapes and Gothicism of Dürer woodcuts which he transformed into fairy kingdoms; or he transposed the elaborate borders of fifteenth- and sixteenth-century illustrated books, and above all borrowed from Japanese prints, with their spare spaces, bold flat colours and striking perspectives. But as with Rackham and many other colleagues, the First World War caused Robinson's career to begin to ebb, and the commissions dried up. Between 1905 and 1909 he had illustrated some 39 books, but since such work was not considered vital to the war effort, he found himself returning to illustrated journalism to support his large family. Even after the war, however, his popularity diminished and like Rackham, he turned to gallery painting and moved out of London to a cottage in Buckinghamshire, where he painted for the Royal Academy, the Royal Institute of Painters in Water Colours (he was created a member in 1932), and for provincial exhibitions in Liverpool, Glasgow and Bristol. He died in 1937, the forever cheerful Bohemian, as he regarded himself. His brother William Heath Robinson eulogised that fantasy and the love of life that had dominated his brother's long and distinguished career: 'There was always something of youth and of being on holiday about Charles'.[44]

THE ENCHANTMENT OF NATURE

WITH THE RISE OF THE WEALTHY Edwardian middle classes came a yearning for escape from the horrors of industrialisation and the urban sprawl that accompanied it. Many felt the resulting growth of the suburbs that encircled the cities and spread into the landscape greatly threatened the true English countryside. As such it was pure sacrilege, for the countryside harboured the escapist virtues of a golden arcadia, the 'Land of Lost Content' which every educated city dweller longed to embrace. Excursions and guidebooks, manuals of nature study and country travel filled the railway bookshops and helped to fuel this new rural religion. It preached the benefits of country walks, while the open fields and country lanes were the essential 'outdoor sitting rooms'. This inspired the creation of the National Trust in 1895, founded to preserve lands rejected by the gentry as unsuitable for their sporting events, and more importantly gave rise to a middle-class fascination with nature. *Country Life* magazine appeared on the newsstands in 1897, offering a voyeuristic peek at vanishing country house life and the much vaunted life of the country gentry, from which many of the aspiring middle classes sought solace and a role model. And when life became hard, when this country idyll was debased by industrialism or the First World War threatened all that was rurally sacred, thoughts turned towards preservation, to the endearing lure of A. E. Housman's 'blue remembered hills', to the ruralist-themed poetry of the War poets, to the music of Elgar and Vaughan Williams, to the warnings by Kenneth Grahame in the *National Observer* extolling the charms of the countryside under threat from the suburbs, and to the raft of publications which reminded soldiers and civilians alike that, 'They'll always be an England/ While there's a country lane./ Wherever there's a cottage small/ Beside a field of grain.'

Enterprising publishers viewed this new ruralist marketplace as untapped treasure, a rich seam from which to produce well-illustrated escapist volumes inspired by the beauty and diversity of Mother Nature for a jaded urban public. It is not surprising that when Kenneth Grahame first published *The Wind in the Willows* in 1908, a misguided *Times* book critic, obviously hoping for more appealing naturalist accuracy, dismissed the tale as ultimately disappointing because 'as a contribution to natural history the book is negligible'. Clearly there was a real thirst for natural knowledge, however superficial, and if a book could inspire, especially with illustrations fired by the beauty of nature, then there was a ready market for it. Fortunately the Detmold twins emerged at this time, and, as a result, these two remarkable talents set the highest benchmarks for nature illustration, standards which have seldom been bettered today.

The Detmold Twins

Indeed, the Detmold brothers, Charles Maurice (known professionally as Maurice) and Edward Julius (cats 77–78) created some of the most original illustrated nature books and prints of the period. From the start, these teenage prodigies stunned their public with their understanding and assured, meticulous draughtsmanship of the natural world. They first made an impact with a joint collaboration volume, *Pictures from Birdland*, with its 24 luminous colour plates published by J. M. Dent in 1899. Then followed solo virtuoso performances by Edward, the orientalist, whose sensitive illustrations to Maurice Maeterlinck's *The Life of the Bee* (1911) borrowed from a delicate Japanese-inspired aesthetic to set new parameters in nature drawing. This was followed by his *Twenty-Four Nature Pictures* (1919), again published by Dent; and finally the more specialized Fabre's

Book of Insects (1921), which challenged even the most enthusiastic entomologist with its cold, surrealist insect portraits painted in high definition colours. In the end, the Detmolds were, for a generation of enthusiasts, the supreme masters of nature in art.

The Detmold twins were born in Putney, west London in 1883. While living with their uncle guardian, they experimented with drawings of animals and, while they were largely self-taught, they gained much from visits to London Zoo and the Natural History Museum. Their charming watercolour of peacocks was perhaps inspired by such visits, and when they collaborated in this fashion it remains a mystery just who painted and drew what on each work (cat. 6). Once their work was shown in public, they were soon declared child geniuses and allowed to exhibit at the Royal Academy at the impressive age of just thirteen. Like their compatriot Beardsley, they were much admired by the famed old guard artist Sir Edward Burne-Jones, who was a real judge of young talent and immediately recognised something remarkable when he met the two fourteen-year-olds in 1897: 'I've met with two geniuses. Of course there's no knowing whether anything may come of it, but they might be a great comfort in the future.' He admired their painting of a stag beetle – 'every hair is done, and the light upon it and the shadows cast on it and all the flatnesses and every kind of shape of it' – and a drawing of a brass pot with 'all the room reflected in it,' which allowed him to conclude: 'There's no knowing where this gift comes from, it's very wonderful. They've got every equipment for being very great artists indeed.'[45]

The praises continued, notably from the influential collector and print critic Campbell Dodgson, who wrote a thorough illustrated survey of their prints in 1910. In it, he claimed the two precocious brothers 'seemed as one soul divided between two bodies, inspired by the same ideal, using the same means of expression, possessing the same quickness of eye and deftness of hand.'[46] The twins then entered the most extraordinary phase of their careers. Inseparable in life and in art, they bought a printing press and began experimenting with animal etchings, creating collaboratively the etchings of birds, fish and mammals which made them famous. They produced these prints in a set of eight proofs for a portfolio, which, when published in 1898, quickly sold out. Others they exhibited at London's Royal Institute of Painters in Watercolour, the English Art Club, and the International Exhibition in Kensington. These were recognised masterpieces of printmaking deemed even more remarkable for having been created at such a young age. The prints soon attracted collectors and influential admirers: 'The "Long-Eared Bat"… in technical execution is the finest and most wonderful of all,' according to their devoted champion Dodgson. 'It was drawn in pencil by Edward, etched chiefly by Maurice, and bitten-in by Edward. No reproduction could render successfully the wonderful lightness of the thin lines, so subtly adapted to every variety of texture, bone, fur, and skin.'[47] In all, ten such prints were produced between 1899 and 1905. 'The Hornbill' shown here was issued in colour and uncoloured editions and indicates the delicacy

of their perceptions of birds (cat. 79).

The Detmold formula was, however, more than mere imitation of nature. According to their recent biographer, their animals were not just specimens of life seen from a human point of view; using their acute understanding of the forces of nature, they created the mythology and harshness of the natural world. A Detmold composition contained more realism and was a less romanticised approach to nature; their animals 'were strong and fierce, filling the page and often fixing the viewer with eyes that stare aggressively back… The pictures often contain both hunter and prey, the surroundings of crooked trees or rugged landscape all add to the feeling of elemental nature.'[48] The first of two book collaborations, *Pictures from Birdland*, published in 1898 when the twins were just sixteen, was filled with early nature drawings to accompany their guardian uncle's rhymes and was followed by a very successful exhibition of 51 animal watercolours, etchings and chromolithographs at the Fine Art Society in 1900. Their winning formula was most apparent in their second collaborative volume, Rudyard Kipling's *The Jungle Book* (1903), in which their bold jungle compositions and strong emotive subjects transformed the exotic children's tale that has become an illustrated classic, reprinted numerous times today (cats 80–81). Always looking for new horizons and challenges, the twins also produced stained glass designs at this time in a similar distinctive exotic and oriental mode, which prefigured Edward's later work of the 1920s.

On the strength of these remarkable prints, which relied upon the mastery of colour inks hand wiped across the etched metal plate ('à la poupée') to produce the unique effects that exploited the variable, unstable and unrepeatable qualities of expert printmaking, the twins were elected associates of the Royal Society of Painter Etchers in 1905. By this time they had produced a remarkable body of work totalling about 60 etchings. Characteristically, once they succeeded in a field they turned elsewhere for new challenges: they immediately resigned from the Society, having resolved to abandon etching – after producing one final plate, 'Peacocks', in Christmas 1905. Nevertheless critical praise continued as admirers marvelled at their skill, comparing their meticulous drawings to the famed nature watercolours of Dürer. Over the next two years, they explored other printmaking techniques and produced a number of aquatints and lithographs. All this time they continued to share their childhood home with their uncle in Hampstead. There on 9 April 1908 a terrible tragedy occurred, when the obsessively sensitive Maurice was found dead, having committed suicide with chloroform after first putting the family cats to sleep in preparation for a planned holiday. He left only a brief, cryptic note on the mantelpiece for his distraught brother and artistic soulmate to ponder the rest of his life: 'This is not the ending of life. I have expressed through my physical means all that they are capable of expressing and I am to lay them aside.'

Edward was deeply shaken but, intent upon continuing his own artistic career, and to help forget the tragedy, he poured himself into his own work, notably illustrating a new edition of *The Fables of Aesop* which appeared in 1909, followed by the *Second Jungle Book* in 1910 and Maeterlinck's *Life of the Bee* the year after. Many saw in these solo productions a lack of selectivity, an absence of the precious atmosphere which had been a hallmark of the twins' work. Such criticisms were crushing blows and they soon took their toll on the equally sensitive Edward, who gradually turned reclusive. Crippled by doubt, his output declined over the next few years. Apart from *Twenty-Four Nature Pictures* in 1919, and W. H. Hudson's *Birds in Town and Village*, it was not until the 1920s that he produced more noteworthy books. In his best, he illustrated Fabre's *Book of Insects* (1921), a near-surreal investigation of the world of creepy-crawlies. His colour palette turned more bizarre, vibrant and luminescent, displaying, in a series of nearly 30 uncharacteristic loose etchings of camels and desert scenes in 1923–24, more than a touch of the exotic orientalism with which he had earlier experimented. The influence of the Near and Far East now became an obsession, although he would never visit either region. This imaginary orient he fused with a delicate super-realism in his version of *The Arabian Nights*, published by Hodder and Stoughton in 1922. The original twelve large, majestic watercolours for the book's plates were expertly printed from his own intricate designs, heightened by borders in elaborate motifs painted to emulate Persian and Indian illuminated miniatures (cat. 82). They also marked the end of Edward's intense, meticulously drawn study of nature in favour of an imaginary, more introverted, fantastical view of life: he had taken refuge from the real world that he had once delighted in with his beloved brother, and escaped into the safety of his fertile imagination.

By the early 1920s Edward's career as a notable printmaker had come to an end, and with the decline in his art went his spirit. In 1921 he bravely attempted to describe his testament in a simple volume, *Life*, for which he had high hopes and in which, without illustrations and printed only on one side of the page, he offered sombre, philosophical meditations on existence, pervaded by a mood of deep pessimism. They were 'the fruits of self-overcoming,' as he sought a more timeless and transcendent world. Sadly the book proved a critical failure; *The Times* greeted it with a bitter scorn which would wound the deeply sensitive Edward for the rest of his life. Nevertheless, he persevered with his proselytising and published two further volumes, this time anonymously, entitled *Selflessness* (1922) and *Greater Things and a Greater than Things* (1923). Moreover, he withdrew from public life and moved to the countryside where he lived reclusively in Montgomeryshire for the next three decades, with his sister and her artist husband, and his long-standing friend, the musician and avid cricketer Harold Hulls. There he turned hermit, the locals never catching even a glimpse of him, while he remained a self-imposed prisoner in his studio. He painted watercolours and made prints that he tried to sell locally (cats 86–88). These were sad, uninspired works of what he obviously thought were easy, saleable subjects, especially birds and flowers, painted in a cloying colour palette with waxen surfaces 'which seem on second glance to be pervaded by a deathly and petrified air,' according to a recent critic.[49] The tigers and goldfish subjects were especially bizarre (cats 83, 87–88). Then in July 1956, after a bout of despair at what he called 'this blood-drenched civilisation', he chose to follow his brother's example and take his own life by shooting himself. It was a tragic end to a brilliant career: Edward Detmold, artist and philosopher, died a sad and ultimately forgotten 73-year-old man, alone in his remote studio surrounded by the vast numbers of works he could no longer sell.

INTERNATIONAL ENCHANTMENT

WITH THE BURGEONING OF the colour gift book market, publishers were anxious to find artists talented enough to provide new and saleable illustrations. Many turned abroad, to foreign-trained art students who, at the turn of the century, descended upon England from the continent hopeful of a career in the fine arts. Artists like the Hungarian Willy Pogany, the Frenchman Edmund Dulac, the Dane Kay Nielsen and the outrageous German Alastair all brought their own unique brand of enchantment to the English marketplace and some were rewarded handsomely for their creations.

Willy Pogany

One of the more successful immigrant artists was the Hungarian émigré Willy Pogany, born William Andrew Pogany (fig. 15). Born in Hungary in 1882, he had a clear talent for drawing. After studying in Budapest and Munich, he moved to Paris, where he submitted caricatures to various popular magazines, before stopping off in London en route to what he believed would be a successful career in America. In London the entrepreneurial publisher George Harrap quickly recognized Pogany's potential; Harrap believed his illustrations might successfully compete with the lucrative productions of his publishing rival Hodder and Stoughton — especially their own emigrant protégé, the popular Edmund Dulac. Young Pogany, who had only planned to stay in Edwardian London for a few weeks to earn enough for his passage, ended up staying ten highly successful years. His numerous commissions included a volume of Hungarian fairy tales, as well as several George Harrap publications, such as *The Rubaiyat of Omar Khayyam* (1909; a limited white vellum-bound edition of 25 copies, and a morocco gilt edition of 525 copies). This one volume set the standards for further similarly produced Pogany gift book

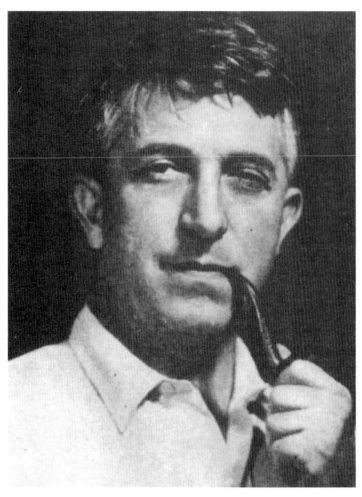

Fig. 15: Willy Pogany.

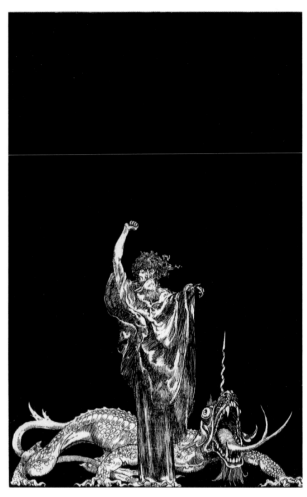

Fig. 16: Illustration from Pogany's *The Rime of the Ancient Mariner* (1910).

volumes, like his influential *The Rime of the Ancient Mariner* (1910; fig. 16), *Lohengrin* (1913; cats 94–95), as well as various children's titles like *The Children in Japan* (1915).

However it was Pogany's *Rime of the Ancient Mariner*, with his 20 tipped-in colour plates and seventeen full-page illustrations with decorated borders and violet and light green backgrounds, that raised the bar on printing standards. This one book alone was 'a *tour de force* of printing both in the quality of the colour and in the elegance of the total design,' according to one recent critic; 'the printer's skill has allowed the artist to use extremely subtle changes in colour and tone to heighten the sense of fantasy and mystery'.[50] Following such successes Pogany eventually produced more than a hundred volumes which, with his inspired talent for the decorative, especially for filling a space, modulating colour and line on tinted paper, found even greater favour with the proponents of the new vogue for Art Deco design.

Pogany was not a British citizen – although he had married a British woman while he worked in London – and with the start of the First World War he decided finally to emigrate to America. There he easily found work and recognition among the many noted New York publishers who were not

as seriously affected by wartime economies. He quickly flourished and was allowed to turn his many talents not only to book illustration (he even produced designs for an American edition of *Alice in Wonderland* in 1929), magazine illustration (like his rival Dulac, he worked on covers for Hearst's *American Weekly*), and mural painting in noted New York landmark buildings (later he painted one for William Randolph Hearst's California home), but also to stage set and costume designs for the New York theatre, including the Metropolitan Opera. Then, when the lucrative world of film beckoned in about 1930, he moved to Hollywood, where, alongside his newest artistic challenges like architecture (he designed houses, hotels and swimming pools) and sculpture, he began to work in the film studios, becoming a film art director for Warner's First National Studios. 'I am always working hard, because it is great fun and hard work to be an artist,' he confessed in 1934. Like many of his fellow émigré artist colleagues – for instance, Kay Nielsen – he ultimately found Hollywood too draining and returned to New York, where he died on 30 July 1955. But even then his influence among the book-buying public persisted, not only in America but also in Britain. In fact, long after his emigration to America his English publications were still reprinted numerous times: his *Rubaiyat of Omar*

Khayyam alone was reprinted almost annually and was still in print in 1961. Even today Willy Pogany's influence remains a potent reminder of the artist's necessity to change with the times. He belongs in the pantheon of talented early twentieth-century decorative masters, although his reputation today survives mostly in America, where he thrived as one of the period's legendary artist chameleons.

Edmund Dulac

With the rise of internationalism in the arts, the superficialities and simple, stark design aesthetic of the Art Deco style was born. It arose out of a popular dissatisfaction with the gloomy decadence of the Art Nouveau designers who, until World War One, had dominated the English decorative arts. Slowly, during and after the war, with the dawn of the Modern Age came a yearning for a truly modern national art style, one suggested by the clean lines and spare concepts of the Scottish architect designer Charles Rennie Mackintosh and his continental colleague Josef Hoffman. Moreover, this experimental atmosphere nurtured a new and international generation of illustrators and designers, artists like the hugely successful Edmund Dulac and his rival, Kay Nielsen. They slowly abandoned the current vogue for linear illustrated narratives (Dulac had first embraced the British Art Nouveau line of Beardsley, while Nielsen had been inspired by the purely decorative folk art traditions) and willingly experimented with pictorial space, surface pattern and those purely decorative tenets of the modern style. They borrowed heavily from the orient, the Near East, and the abstract, geometric forms of Africa – which new designers found especially popular for the veneered furniture of the 1920s, coupled with the revival of eighteenth-century exuberances by using ornate gilt swags, curtains and ormolu furniture detailing. Others turned to classical mythology, which greatly influenced Deco sculpture as well as illustration. Above all, it was the attraction of the spare, innovative perspectives of the orient, the simplicity and beauty of the lacquer wares of Japan and China, the opulence and architecture of Egypt and the intricately painted Persian miniatures which helped to create a quite distinctive amalgamation of the purely decorative, the style known today as Art Deco. As displayed here, the fine illustrations of Edmund Dulac and Kay Nielsen sit happily alongside the innovative furniture, textiles, carpets and ceramics which filled the splendid new Art Deco interior. Dulac in fact once designed an entire Japanese-styled Art Deco room complete with furniture of his own creation. It was an international style which emerged by the 1920s as a refreshing new challenge to British design and was enthusiastically embraced by a large public: 'Infinitely adaptable, it gave free reign to the imagination and celebrated the fantasies, fears and desire of people all over the world,' according to the style's most recent chronicler.[51]

Edmund Dulac (fig.17) was a unique figure in this Deco world, a French-born polymath designer and artist of not only delightfully exotic illustrations, but also postage stamps, posters, bank notes, bookplates, playing cards, tapestries, carpets and furniture. He was born near Toulouse on 22 October 1882 and from his teenage years he developed an Anglophile's love of the arts, taking Beardsley and Walter Crane as his mentors. At art school, first at the École des Beaux Arts, then the prestigious Académie Julian (where Kay Nielsen attended two years later), he was known as 'l'anglais' for his obsessive love of everything English – as an art student he constantly dressed in English tweeds. At the age of just 22, he was convinced his future lay abroad and he left France for the artistic opportunities of his beloved England; he never returned and became a British subject seven years later.

In London Dulac first struggled with saleable Beardsley-inspired inventions for magazines, while spending his leisure time experimenting and searching for his own marketable style. As a proud Anglophile, his first major book illustration commission was appropriately twelve watercolour plates for an edition of that very English classic, *Jane Eyre*, which was published in the spring of 1905 by J. M. Dent. Dulac had been given just three months to complete the commission, and he rose to the challenge admirably. In fact, on its publication he was introduced to the Leicester Galleries firm of Ernest Brown & Phillips (by his future rival Arthur Rackham, whose own gallery career had been launched there), which was responsible for inaugurating the careers of many of the period's finest artist-illustrators. Impressing all with his meticulous detail and fine technique for reproduction, Dulac was suggested for a new edition of *Stories from the Arabian Nights* and it was this commission, published in 1907, and the subsequent exhibition of the 50 original watercolours at the Leicester Galleries, which secured his reputation as an inventive new illustrative force in the publishing world (cats 98–101). He rose to become master of the colourfully foreign at a time when the appeal of the Near East was a refreshing new aesthetic. In true gift book style, Hodder and Stoughton launched Dulac's *Arabian Nights* in various editions so that it would serve as a fantasy companion to the then famously popular Arthur Rackham's *Peter Pan* of the previous year. With publication in October to catch the Christmas market, sales soared and a reprint had to be ordered in November, in time for the Leicester Galleries' exhibition of the book's originals, which sold out immediately. Such was the influence of this one book that Dulac used it to inspire future magazine work in America, and as late as 1925 he consented to redraw text images and backgrounds from the book for the first full-length animated German film, *The Adventures of Prince Ahmed*, directed by Lotte Reiniger.

Thus began an annual book collaboration between Dulac, his publisher Hodder and Stoughton and the Leicester Galleries that lasted until 1916, and then, after wartime economies took their toll, again in 1918 and 1920, when two books appeared in each of those years. Dulac's career was sealed as an illustrator of quality collectors' editions, which were often sold out on publication, as well as the more affordable trade editions, and his output of some 116 titles made him a household figure in countless middle-class homes throughout the world. Indeed his work was reprinted in America, while editions appeared in French, German, Dutch, Italian,

Spanish, Russian and Portuguese. *The Arabian Nights* was followed by other classics including *The Tempest* (1908), *The Rubaiyat of Omar Khayyam* (1909), *Stories from Hans Andersen* (1911), *The Bells and other Poems* by Edgar Allan Poe (1912), *Princess Badoura* (1913), *Sinbad the Sailor and other stories from the Arabian Nights* (1914), and *Edmund Dulac's Fairy Book* (1916).

Just what was the secret of Dulac's remarkable success? As a foreigner working in England, he brought his own unique vision to the world of illustrative publishing, which had previously been dominated by a staunchly English, purely illustrative and heavily narrative style, with its accent upon clarity and most of all black and white line. Dulac loved to mix styles, taking inspiration from the world around him; he introduced subtlety, painted with far more exotic colours and created his own language, drawing upon influences from the Far and the Near East. Fortunately colour printing technologies by the 1900s had evolved beyond mere imitation and could capture through the three-colour process the delicacy of Dulac's watercolour originals. His chief rival was Rackham, whose Gothic fantasies were steeped in a Germanic medievalism which strongly contrasted with Dulac's more colourful Asian themes. Dulac's vision grew out of a more refined world of orientalising, which greatly appealed to a younger audience tired of gloomy historicism. From childhood, Dulac's love of oriental painting, ceramics and style greatly influenced his approach to his decorative design and illustration: 'He would have chosen some dream city of the Orient for his birthplace, a Persian princess for his mother, an artist of the Ming Dynasty for his father,' remarked an American admirer on the eve of his first American exhibition.[52]

Despite the commercial pressures of publishing, Dulac was a perfectionist, and each illustration was worked upon countless times, using numerous tracings to create the exact atmosphere he demanded of it. If a flaw occurred even after several days' work on a drawing, he willingly scrapped it and started again – such was his belief in perfection. Indeed Dulac was primarily a creator of carefully crafted and researched environments, culled from his large knowledge of art history and antiquities. His signature style was, until 1912, what he called 'nocturnes' or what critics have called his 'Blue Period'. His biographer Colin White best explains how masterful these atmospheric blue-tinted watercolours were: 'The *Arabian Nights* gave Dulac an opportunity to indulge in his nocturnes; the softness of the gleam of moonlight on stone, or on shadowy figures, and his use of ultramarine, indigo and Prussian blue, mingled with purples and violets, brought to the illustrations the calm and mystery of Eastern nights. Textures were already important to him. He could capture magnificently the veining and slight translucency of a marble floor, and occasionally borrowed a technical trick from photography and over-damped his paper so as to blur the foreground and bring the eye into apparent focus on the action mid-stage; similarly he would bring out highlights with great delicacy, as in a forehead glistening with perspiration, achieved by dabbing the wet colour with a sponge or blotting paper and a

Fig. 17: Edmund Dulac, c.1915.

damp brush. He also used little dots of light to produce a contrast against a background of darker surfaces. Starting naturally with stars against a deep clear sky, he went on to the sparkle of jewels on garments… and, in his later work, isolated points of reflection on a leaf or stalks as the Impressionists had done.'[53] A further example of his mastery of the azure tones appeared in the *Tempest* illustrations in 1908 (cats 103–104). Always the supreme perfectionist, there is a wonderful story of a visitor to his studio who tried to brush off a bead of water on his drawing board, only to discover it had been painted there - such was the perfectionist skill of Dulac's brush.

This 'Blue Period' came to a gradual end with his illustrations to Edgar Allan Poe's *The Bells and Other Poems*, 1912. Here was a book of macabre tales filled with images of 'cold despair', according to the critics. The ethereal moonlit Blue Period world had now turned sour, with washed-out blues and greys, where heads float in space, women swoon, sleep or die, men, sunk in despair, contemplate the infinite (cats 111–112). Nevertheless, the deluxe edition sold out and was oversubscribed, while overall trade sales proved heavy. And yet Dulac yearned for a new style: unwilling to be typecast, he turned away from sharp definition and bold colour to a more placid, atmospheric world of pastel tones and faded outline. His skies were made by dabbing with a large brush, lightly blotting each section before applying the next, to produce a soft, mottled surface resembling shot silk. Everything was imbued with a lighter cast, 'the texture of tinted, frosted glass' and gradually cloudless skies became patterned shapes, painted under the influence of his beloved Persian miniatures or using shorthand for figures in a landscape derived from Chinese painting. Perspective bowed to Eastern ideals where a single picture plane gave way to overall diversity and symbolism.

Colour took on new importance. Although he was not a willing or seasoned traveller, he was inspired by a Mediterranean cruise in 1913 which proved a turning point in his search for a new style. From aboard ship he stared into the Aegean Sea, transfixed by the colours which he recorded poetically in his journal: the sunset at Brindisi was 'a truly oriental manner with a fire of pneumatic rays around its head, the moon on the left powders the water with silver very charmingly'. Nearing the islands off Corfu, where sailing boats were like 'shells or butterflies', the islands were 'strongly reminiscent of Hokusai drawings, spotted like leopard skins and streaked like zebras, buff, golden and silvery opalescent.' But here especially, it was the sea's colour that left him transfixed: 'Blue – the only blue, a blue to make you drunk.' Poetically he tried to describe his newfound fascination with the natural world: 'The sea is charmingly like golden moiré, a slight mist on the horizon, ahead cerulean. Behind us the sun is being wrapped up in a changing cloth of gold, deep orange and light metallic green dropping purply incense. On the one side the foam makes designs of molten lapis lazuli.'

This voyage strengthened Dulac's oriental vision. Here he witnessed for the first time scenes which he had earlier only imagined for the street markets and Arabian settings of his *Arabian Nights* drawings. These he soon adopted, using a more subtle colouring and borrowing from the intricacies of Persian miniatures for his next book, *Sinbad the Sailor and Other Stories from the Arabian Nights*, 1914 (cats 115–118). In Greece he was astonished how 'the town looked quite Arabic, flat roofs, palms, cubes of all shades of white, blue and ochres, with Orientals in their red fez and baggy trousers.' It was a place of absolute delight, 'where the sentimental traveller can give himself up to memories of a graceful past'. In the marketplace in Tunis, where he made brief costume studies and saw a snake charmer and a belly dancer, he experienced his drawings come to life, 'with the merchants sitting in their small, painted niches, the silks; shoes; clothes and tattooed Bedouin beggars; the walls covered in Islamic decorations; the odours of pepper, cedarwood, and pitch, arcades supported by columns in twists of green, yellow, and red.'[54]

During World War One, Dulac sensed his career might suffer and, like his colleagues Rackham, Pogany, and Nielsen, he turned his talents to other avenues for the war effort. He created stamp designs denoting the five wartime virtues: Courage, Hope, Victory, Faith and Assistance. He also joined his illustrator colleagues and contributed illustrations to the numerous publishers' charity volumes like *Princess Mary's Gift Book* (1914), *King Albert's Book* (1914) and *Edmund Dulac's Picture-Book for the Red Cross* (1915; cat. 120). Each of these distinctive volumes had been supported by contributions from the period's most famous writers and artists, and were produced by enterprising newspapers and book publishers anxious to 'do their bit' for the troops. In addition, with publishers rationing their wartime publications, Dulac had to find alternative sources of income. He turned to the more lucrative art of portrait painting, as well as to his long-standing love of caricature. Over the years he had enjoyed drawing his friends and their associates in clever parodies of English drawing room behaviour, which puzzled and bemused the dapper Frenchman. A charming social animal who loved the social whirl of London life and the gossip of the drawing room, Dulac revelled in observing his colleagues from a distance. Famous friends like Charles Ricketts and Charles Shannon, his special friend W. B. Yeats and their circle often featured in his delightfully wicked parodies of wartime life in London. He exhibited six of these for the first time in 1914 (cat. 30).

As the war dragged on he produced one of his last annual gift books, *Edmund Dulac's Fairy Book: Fairy Tales of the Allied Nations* (1916), in which he attempted to emulate a diverse number of nationalistic styles in each drawing. It was clearly a labour of love and, despite fears that he was losing his sight in one eye, he persevered and the book was published to great acclaim, although it was issued in a much smaller collectors' edition of just 350 copies. His new style now emerged in its full glory, with its bold opaque colours and a dependency upon a drawing's overall richness of effect rather than mere individual detail: the lessons of his Mediterranean cruise had been well learnt. At this time Dulac also began to theorise about the role of the illustrator, and in an essay, 'Modes of Thought and Aesthetic Expression' for *Discovery* magazine, he pointed out his views in the strongest terms: 'The end result of objective imitative art is nothing less than coloured photography,' while he preferred the freer expression of space without the constraints of Western perspective. Here was the influence of his love of oriental perspective. Indeed he had recently moved studios and he transformed his new home with its more spacious rooms into an homage to the orient: the walls were hung with Chinese paintings and a series of Japanese prints showing Europeans in 1860s costumes, while his desk was piled high with Japanese brushes and the small lidded ivory oriental ceramic pots for his colours. Everywhere were the chairs, tables, cupboards, radio case and adjustable lamps that he had designed under the spell of the orient. By this time the oriental aesthetic inspired not only his books but also his most recent stage and costume designs. While the popular Russians like Leon Bakst and the Ballets Russes, who had taken London by storm in 1919, were great influences, Dulac's theatre designs included a recent production of Japanese Noh-inspired sets (which he completed with his friend W. B. Yeats, in collaboration with Ezra Pound as the stage manager), a clear sign his love of the orient might pervade every new commission. Moreover, when he was asked to design interiors, he turned to themes familiar from his book illustrations: an especially successful commission was to transform the Albert Hall into an Arabian fantasy for the Chelsea Arts Ball. Later he created an oriental Art Deco masterpiece by designing orientalist-inspired furniture, wall coverings and lighting for the Cathay lounge of the liner *The Empress of Britain*.

By the 1920s, Dulac was financially crippled. Dulac, Rackham and Nielsen each found his career in the doldrums as their particular brand of lavishly produced gift book was no longer fashionable or economical to a nation struggling to recover from years of wartime hardship. Characteristically, and true to a long tradition of artists in hardship, they all turned to America, where to their great relief they generally found willing, wealthy and adoring patrons. In 1924 Dulac began a long and remunerative collaboration with William Randolph Hearst's Sunday newspaper colour supplement *The American Weekly*. Here between 1924 and 1951 he created 106 full-page cover illustrations at the average rate of ten per year. (cat. 122). For these he was paid handsomely and he retained the copyright and the originals, the latter of which he sold for $250 each. True, they were pure commercial art, but even here Dulac imbued each drawing with a conscious sense of perfection, either in superb colour, innovative design or composition. While his relationship with the Americans was not always easy, he embraced this lifeline and remained dedicated to his tasks. Other commissions followed, like the three volumes he created for the Limited Editions Club of New York, notably his meticulously conceived version of Pushkin's *The Golden Cockerel* (1950), issued in a strictly limited edition of 1500 copies signed by Dulac. These he juggled alongside more commercial work, like the stamps and bank notes for the Free French in 1940, followed by British royal commissions: a stamp design for Queen Elizabeth which he carefully adopted from royal photographs, and later her Coronation stamp bearing both heads of the new Queen and the late King in 1953.

It is interesting to view Dulac's career in light of his fascinating character. Like Rackham, he was totally self-effacing, and rarely mentioned his art in public despite his international reputation. As an illustrator, he accepted his role as secondary to the fine art painter: 'We illustrators are the middle-classes in art'. He condemned the popular myth of the starving Bohemian artist whose purpose in life was the sole worship of beauty: 'Beauty is not a word that is ever used in polite society,' he sniffed. He left no Universal Message, and yet after nearly a half century of perfectionism he was eulogised as 'a collectors' artist' and 'a man in love with craftsmanship': 'To him a full life was one in which an attempt was made to accomplish everything; to know everything that had contributed to the civilization of man, and if sometimes he was impatient with the world it was merely an overflow of the impatience within himself and a reflection of an inner urge to worry a task to its limits. Time was always the enemy,' his biographer concluded. 'Indeed, he considered himself "a diverger", a gregarious person wanting the stimulus and conflict of other minds.'[55] With his energetic personality, Dulac was passionate about life and explored its

numerous facets wherever he lived; in his early thirties he kept gymnastic rings in his studio and performed stunts and workouts in between bouts of intense painting. He was an expert revolver shot and a dedicated musician, who played the bamboo flute – which he made himself – with his nose. He loved dressing up all his life, especially in the oriental costumes he designed for himself and his wife, and he showed a special talent for designing and applying makeup. He also embraced spiritualism with his second wife, the novelist Helen Beauclerk, whose works he illustrated. They lived in some bohemian splendour in London's Holland Park, their tall townhouse complete with a long back garden punctuated by a Moorish-inspired summer house studio, where Dulac could work, inspired by views of the tall trees from the arched windows. But above all he adored flamenco dancing, and would sweep across the dance floor in elegant moves to the delight of his many friends. Perhaps it was a fitting end then, that Edmund Dulac, the embracer of life, should die, on 25 May 1953, aged 70, after a demonstration of his flamenco prowess to a group of adoring friends: sadly this one last exuberant display brought on the subsequent heart attack and proved to be his final performance.

Kay Nielsen

One of the most influential international émigré artists, who created a remarkable reputation for himself with just five books published in Britain from 1912 to 1930, was Kay Rasmus Nielsen. Born in Copenhagen in 1886, the son of an actor who was theatre manager of the Royal Copenhagen Theatre and a famous actress mother, young Nielsen was greatly influenced by his parents' professions: 'They brought me up in a tense atmosphere of art,' he later recalled of the household filled with noted playwrights and writers like Ibsen, and musicians like Grieg. His parents loved classical French theatre and the local Danish folklore which would in time dominate Nielsen's illustrations. It was a privileged childhood and young Kay was tutored privately from the age of twelve, and by his adoring mother who loved to read her son his native Danish folk tales and legends, while he practised drawing their stirring scenes of errant knights and forlorn maidens in distress. His grandfather loved art as well, and from his travels to the orient he had collected the Japanese prints which, along with his collection of delicate silk Chinese landscape paintings, would greatly inspire the young artist's future work.[56]

By 1904, then aged just seventeen, Nielsen left his native Denmark for art studies in Paris, first at the prestigious Académie Julian under J. P. Laurens, then at the Collarossi Academy. Driven by ambition, he spent his spare moments experimenting with illustrations to his most favourite poets like Verlaine and Heine, as well as the stories of his beloved compatriot Hans Andersen. By this time those art students intent upon commercial careers in illustration realised that the best opportunities for advancement lay in England, which was notoriously the home of artistic experimentation and a burgeoning publishing industry hungry for new talent. 'It was the fastidiousness, the affectation, but more particularly the unwholesome

Fig. 18: Nielsen's 'The Gloomy Thick Wood' from *King Albert's Book* (1914).

excess of the later Beardsley which most captured the imagination of the impulsive and pessimistic young Nielsen,' recalled his first biographer.[57] His English friends much admired a selection of Nielsen's early illustrations done largely in homage to Beardsley, and they urged him to visit London in hope of securing their publication and exhibition. He arrived in 1911 with a portfolio of largely black and white ink fantasy drawings he called 'The Book of Death', which he hoped to exhibit and sell in a London gallery. There was a strong air of Strindbergian angst and painful brooding in these early works, which some found extraordinary coming from an artist of just 26. The haunting narrative of eight drawings was the doomed love of Pierrot: from his fear of losing his beloved ('The Omen'), his separation from her ('Inevitable'), and the poignant scene where the love-lorn Pierrot witnesses her death and entombment ('The Chasm'), in which Nielsen's waif-like Pierrot flings roses into his beloved's sepulchre as he prepares to take his suicidal plunge to join her into the darkness below. This was followed by the more hopeful 'The Vision' and 'Yearning' – in which a distraught Pierrot comes to terms with his loss and struggles with the idea that his love is now a spirit and with him forever – before his eventual death and the drawing that completed the narrative he labelled 'End'.

Success was soon forthcoming after the 'Book of Death' drawings and a selection of similarly emotive compositions inspired by favourite Hans Andersen stories and select Heinrich Heine verses were exhibited at Messrs Dowdeswell Galleries in London's prestigious New Bond Street in July 1912. On the strength of this debut, Nielsen was commissioned by the premier gift book publisher Hodder and Stoughton to illustrate a selection of eighteenth-century tales compiled by Sir Arthur Quiller-Couch entitled *In Powder and Crinoline*. Published the following year, Nielsen's innovative 24 colour plates, including an oval frontispiece, appeared in the bookshops in an elaborately bound expensive limited edition for the collectors' market as well as a cheaper trade edition (cats 123–124). The book quickly secured Nielsen's reputation as a new young talent to watch; his eighteenth-century pastiches were in clear homage to the late Beardsley, yet he seemed to have instilled in each drawing a more generous, colourful exuberance, delighting in pattern, colour and an oriental inventiveness which would in time rival the best of Dulac, Rackham, Pogany and even Harry Clarke. Nielsen's winning formula was derived largely from his beloved folkloric background; he also borrowed from a love of early Italian painting, from the delicate Persian miniatures and Indian and Chinese landscapes which he mixed and borrowed in a process he called 'artistic wandering'. But at this time his greatest debt was still to Beardsley, and he borrowed from his mastery of bold, flat evocative spaces. In time Nielsen wisely tempered this starkness with a more decorative, intricate rococo detailing, placing his figures off-centre or diagonally in the oriental fashion. From the French he derived a 'fashion-plate' simplicity and adopted a startling full-frontal honesty which introduced an added dimension of frankness to his narratives, where the Nielsen women were expertly and elaborately dressed in the intricate confections of the period's finest couturiers.

Always inventive, occasionally playful, Nielsen would throughout his career spice up his compositions by mixing what he considered to be the best of many artistic worlds. In one instance he mysteriously inserted into an elaborate floral and vine border a pair of knitting needles; in another Arabic scene he bizarrely inserted an incongruous Alpine hat complete with expertly drawn pheasant feathers. Favourite subjects and themes recurred, as did various compositional devices like the many columns and pillars which he drew to rise suggestively alongside tempting young maidens. Floral motifs recalled his wife's love of gardening, while his simple outlined 'Tudor-rose' echoed those linear flower motifs of his Scottish rival Jessie King. Silhouettes were a great favourite used by many of the period's best illustrators, notably Arthur Rackham in his later endpaper designs. Being Danish, Nielsen recalled his country's traditions of paper cut-out figures which often decorated the rooms and trees of a Danish Christmas and he adopted the technique for the cut-out animals, birds and floral borders seen in his later *Hansel and Gretel* illustrations (cat. 127). Above all, however, it was the folk motifs which dominated a Nielsen illustration; they were characteristic, sometimes borrowed from elements of various European cultures, but more likely taken from the painted furniture and tapestries and folk art of his beloved Denmark (fig. 18).

Such explorations led Nielsen to the one work which most consider his masterpiece: his 25 evocative colour plates to illustrate the fifteen Scandinavian folk tales compiled in *East of the Sun, West of the Moon, Old Tales from the North*. Again published by Hodder and Stoughton in 1914 in an elaborate white vellum-bound limited edition, this one book captured the spirit of the international age of enchantment (cat. 125). Nielsen mixed a heady brew, combining Russian folk art, Nordic harshness and the finesse of the orient – especially in his Hokusai-inspired rendition of the rolling sea – and in one plate even nodded to his rival, Harry Clarke, with a Gothic tribute to Clarke's own peaked stained windows that he set in a blackened room to illustrate 'On that island stands a church…' The entire project was clearly a labour of love; published on the eve of the First World War, it seemed to strike an escapist chord. With its diverse themes of power, honesty and love, and Nielsen's strong images, it attracted enthusiastic criticism and a large public: 'Above all this collection has the authenticity of felt experience – the scent of the pine forest, the ice of the polar flows, the solitary birch in the arctic waste, the creatures that inhabit the lands of fjord and midnight sun, the heroes of Lied and Saga.'

With this one work Nielsen established himself as a master of an international aesthetic more seductive, rarefied and appealing than any of his rivals. 'What Nielsen offers in his beautiful paintings and book illustrations is not merely an escape from the mindlessness of modern existence. His retreat into a world of childhood fantasy is no innocent indulgence; it is where, like his romantic predecessors, he finds the imagination can conceive of infinite possibility and grasp an alternative vision where hope remains undimmed,' claimed a recent champion.[58] However, artistic success is in large part about timing, and sadly for Nielsen his career took off in the shadows of the impending First World War. Hodder and Stoughton usually issued his books in two lucrative editions, the lavishly presented limited edition in just 500 copies signed and numbered by Nielsen for his devoted book collectors, while a cheaper trade edition usually entered the shops in time for pre-Christmas sales. To augment his income, Nielsen, like his rivals Rackham and Dulac, agreed to sell off the original drawings for their new annual gift book at the London Leicester Galleries; this not only helped to promote a new book but also provided welcome income during a financially strained period in Nielsen's career. Indeed, Nielsen found illustration work was scarce despite his critical success, and he reluctantly returned to Denmark over the wartime period, where he knew he could confidently find work as a stage designer in his father's theatre. He would not in fact publish another illustrated book for ten more years.

While in Denmark, Nielsen poured himself into designing the costumes and sets for the Royal Copenhagen Theatre's lavish productions – many of which could easily have been turned into illustrated volumes, such was Nielsen's characteristic care and thoroughness over each project. Indeed he soon gained celebrity status as a theatrical designer in his native country, which allowed him to live very well, with a country house where he enjoyed a life of some splendour. With his new friend and collaborator Johannes Poulssen, he worked in 1918–22 upon such characteristically romantic productions as *Aladdin* (1919), *Scaramouche* (1922; with a score by Sibelius, illustrated by Nielsen), and *The Poet's Dream*. And yet all the while Nielsen was not willing to abandon illustration altogether; even while he pored over stage and costume designs, he worked intermittently upon a series of lavish and mildly erotic gouache illustrations to a Danish translation by Arthur Christensen of *The Arabian Nights*. The project grew into a delightfully ambitious series of evocative paintings, over which he took exceptional care. Sadly the project languished due to wartime economies and was never published as intended; a reprint of his 20 thirteen-inch-square gouache paintings only appeared 20 years later.[59] But it was clear from this work that even in Nielsen's theatrical exile he refused to abandon his love of his country's folklore. He earnestly believed that folk tales were essential to the lives of all ages – hence the potency of myth, legend and fairy tale – and while they were often peopled by the exotic and the bizarre, it was only in pure folk tales that man's true predicament was effectively and cogently symbolised.

As early as 1912, Nielsen had begun work upon a series of illustrations to his favourite tales by Hans Andersen, and he harboured a strong desire to illustrate a volume of his compatriot's classic stories. It was not until twelve years later that the opportunity arose, when a war-ravaged Britain was now seeking escapist fantasy from the horrors of its immediate past. He produced just twelve colour drawings to illustrate the sixteen Andersen tales in Hodder and Stoughton's *Hans Andersen's Fairy Tales*, published in 1924. (The delay in Nielsen's edition may be due to the fact that his publishers had already issued William Heath Robinson's version of Andersen's tales in 1913 and wished to continue its sales.) Sadly the ten-year period of inactive publishing had taken its toll upon Nielsen's abilities, and this new volume lacked his characteristic inventiveness and care, combining as it did the older, more finished drawings with those less considered he freshly created. Moreover this unevenness and slacking-off of artistic standards was continued the following year, when appeared another patchy volume of illustrated tales, *Hansel and Gretel: Stories from the Brothers Grimm*, which Hodder published in the usual two editions, although this time increasing the limited edition to 600 copies, fetchingly bound in white silken linen decorated in blue and gilt. A French edition of this book followed, covered in paper-wrappers, entitled *Fleur-de-Neige* (Snow White) in a limited edition of 2400 copies, of which 400 were offered in a vellum binding. But such elaborate publisher showmanship for Nielsen's latest work could not jump-start his career or indeed overcome the fact that there was a noticeable falling-off in his technique; with their thinness of colour and unnecessary expansiveness of space, the illustrations severely hindered this book's charm and ultimately its sales.

As the market for Nielsen's illustration work dwindled, with popular taste veering away from his characteristic delicacy of lavishly decorated surfaces using foreign motifs towards the new, more simplistic, geometric, hard-edged Art Deco, many observers heralded the end of what they called the 'Golden Age of Illustration'. His rivals also began to feel the strain of securing commissions and, while Dulac turned to portraiture and Rackham found American patrons, Nielsen was convinced to try one more illustrated volume in England. Sadly it was not a success, with a smaller format and less ambitiously produced. *Red Magic: A Collection of the World's Best Fairy Tales from all Countries*, edited by Romer Wilson and published this time by Jonathan Cape in 1930, included just eight Nielsen colour plates, augmented with 50 black and white page fillers and text decorations; perhaps as a sign of the publisher's lack of confidence or false economies, the truncated production was uncharacteristically issued in just one trade cloth edition, which critics dismissed as 'rather inauspicious' (cat. 128). The heyday of publishers' extravagant production values had clearly passed and with it the healthy careers of the gift book illustrators.

It was clear a change was needed to bolster Nielsen's flagging career, especially now that the 44-year-old artist was married to the delightfully refreshing Ulla, a devoted Danish soulmate 20 years his junior. He turned his sights to the lucrative promises of America, especially to California, where he went with Poulssen to work upon a Hollywood Bowl production of Max Reinhardt's *Everyman*, leaving his young wife in Denmark. Soon opportunities encouraged him, and work was offered by the Walt Disney Studios where he began designs for their animated masterpiece *Fantasia* (he is credited with devising the 'Bald Mountain' sequence and working upon the 'Ave Maria' section). But such work was too demanding for an artist in late middle age; the studio bosses were famous for exhausting even their younger staff with their incessant demands and schedules. Here the meticulous Nielsen was required to produce quick chalk drawings of possible characters and the speed and alien chalk medium grated upon his finer sensibilities. He was, after all, a perfectionist, a master of time-consuming, well-honed and pristine watercolour designs of great intricacy and beauty which could and did take months to complete. Nevertheless he persevered until he eventually fell out with the intrusive Disney bosses over his work on their next feature *The Little Mermaid*, and he left his studio job (although years later when the film appeared he was credited posthumously).

With no work and few prospects he felt understandably despondent, jobless in the fast-paced commercial world of America. When his beloved Ulla joined him at the outbreak of the Second World War, together they struggled with seemingly interminable economies, first from their tiny mortgaged bungalow, and eventually moving to a smaller rented house which they filled with beguiling remnants of their lavish life in the old country. At one stage they devised a plan to rear Cornish game hens to sell to their neighbours and filled the house with young birds, but this never succeeded. Friends rallied round whenever they could, at times offering exotic delicacies like caviar which often seemed cruelly inappropriate when even the barest essentials were so hard to come by. In 1941 Nielsen was asked to design a 3,000-foot mural for a Los Angeles Junior High School, which he called 'The First Spring', and he based his intricate design of animals and flowers upon the biblical arrival of Noah's Ark. This was completed to much critical fanfare: Arthur Miller in the *Los Angeles Times* called it 'one of the most beautiful wall paintings in America'. Then followed a series of morale-deflating events: tragically the school building was to be transformed into government offices, and despite a last-minute campaign to save Nielsen's mural it had to be dismantled. This was so poorly done that, despite objections by Nielsen, it was almost ruined. Upset and angry, he eventually agreed to spend two soul-destroying years restoring it. Another California school mural commission followed, then a church mural altarpiece, but even these occasional commissions failed to quell the Nielsens' financial worries.

The end came slowly as Nielsen fell further into a debilitating poverty and professional obscurity, and with it went all his artistic ambition. A tall, dapper man with aquiline features, he was always well dressed, often in characteristic tweeds. With impeccable manners and a ubiquitous cigarette (amid constant bouts of coughing), he was the much-loved centre of his suburban California neighbourhood, even serving there as 'block warden' during wartime. His devoted wife buoyed his spirits and made valiant efforts to keep their home filled with the pleasures they missed from their homeland, cutting out paper dolls for their Christmas tree and inventing floral decorations. But it was not to be, and after eighteen unfruitful years in America, Kay Nielsen died there a broken and forgotten man in 1957. He was survived by his adoring wife and a beloved French poodle, 'The Little Old Man'. Tributes were few, as his books were long out of print. It was not until the mid-1970s that he was rediscovered in America and most of his books were reprinted there. It was only in 2007 that his Danish compatriots at the GL Holtegaard Museum outside his native Copenhagen held a splendid tribute exhibition. As a fitting monument to this supremely talented artist, an anthology volume perceptively claimed that throughout his career Nielsen had devoted himself to 'the lyrical and the poetical' – concepts which he discovered to his cost were now totally alien to the superficial tastes of the middle of the twentieth century.

Alastair

Hans Henning von Voight, or 'Alastair', was one of Nielsen's more inventive contemporaries, a true European with an intensely rarefied, if not refined approach to illustration which often echoed Nielsen's own carefully crafted work (fig. 19). A mysteriously enigmatic figure, who was largely self-taught, Alastair was obsessed with decadence and transvestism and above all was a true disciple of Beardsley's more obsessive traits. Born in Karlsruhe in 1887, to mixed English, Spanish and Russian ancestry, he lived mostly in

Fig. 19: Alastair.

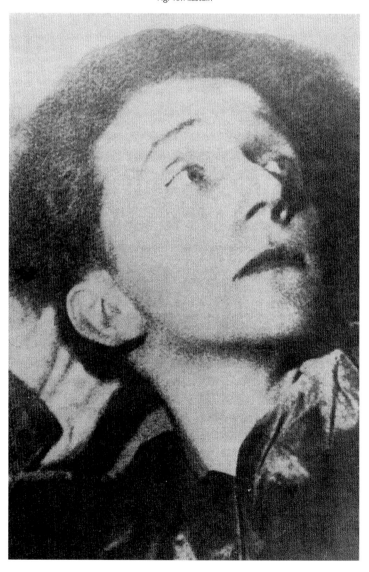

Germany, although he developed a small but devoted following in England, especially after John Lane issued an anthology of his early designs as *Forty-Three Drawings by Alastair* 'with a note of exclamation' (sic) by Robert Ross, Beardsley's executor. Six years later appeared his edition of Oscar Wilde's *The Sphinx* (1920), followed by illustrations to such decadent masterpieces as Walter Pater's *Sebastian Van Storck* (1927), the Abbe Prevost's *Manon Lescaut* (1928; cat. 131), and a particularly eerie edition of Edgar Allan Poe's horrific tale *The Fall of the House of Usher* (1928).

Alastair's style borrowed heavily from the rococo exuberance and erotic suggestiveness of his beloved Beardsley, although, being self-taught, his drawings lacked the finesse and overall finish of his master. His main weakness lay in his attenuated figures with their cursory China-doll facial features. Condemned as decadent by his critics, he thrived upon his imagination and inventions, like the lasciviousness of his women, dressing them in gowns of snakeskin tightness and wonderfully inventive floral fantasies which rival even today's more outrageous couturiers. Alastair's world was one of excesses, of sensuality, the love of the perverse and above all the feminine. His drawing of Messalina, the vampish character Beardsley had given memorable form to years earlier, became for Alastair in Swinburne's *Masque of Queen Bersabe* a masterful tiered confection of ruffles and lace. His Herodias in his series of drawings to Wilde's *Salome* (a favourite subject which Alastair drew in several sets) was a pointillist homage to the exotic Arabian sensibilities pioneered by Dulac and Nielsen (cat. 132). It is fascinating to compare Nielsen's unpublished *Arabian Nights* gouaches to Alastair's imagined Arabia. Finally, his sympathetic interpretation of Wilde's *The Picture of Dorian Grey*, with a feminised Dorian, waif-like and sickly, asleep in a plumed canopy bed beneath a counterpane of chrysanthemums and thorns, was a masterstroke of decadent invention.

There was also a strong borrowing from the Ballets Russes, especially in his exotic colour sense, which he carried into his own theatre designs for sets, costumes and even posters. A reclusive figure with an uncanny resemblance to Pierrot, Alastair lived surrounded by mounds of sensuous lilies and a selection of carefully placed fine antique furniture, being always a slave to his aesthetic. By the 1920s that aesthetic had reached America, where a group of his drawings appeared at the Weyhe Gallery in New York in 1925. A second book helped to launch his American debut, *Fifty Drawings by Alastair*, published in New York by Alfred Knopf with an introduction by Carl Van Vechten. But like his contemporaries, for an artist with such refined sensibilities and such a limited approach to his art, he discovered in time work was difficult to find. A new volume of drawings to Laclos's scandalous *Les Liaisons Dangereuses* appeared in 1929, which were created in a sense of supreme occasion, his characters emotive and tantalising (cat. 129) but in later years he drew only for exhibitions – in five years he had completed 150 drawings for the galleries.

In the end Alastair remained an enigmatic puzzle, a curious mixture of petulance, childishness and anger, who refused to be pinned down and was always on the move. Bright and extremely literate, he wrote articles on Dandyism, translated and wrote treatises in florid prose for numerous magazines. He lived a long life, and when he finally died in 1969, even to those who had known him he remained a secretive legend. His legacy remains a sheaf of exquisite drawings and a few magically illustrated volumes. He once wrote, 'Time is quite unreal, a stroll in false perspective,' and he even attempted to capture his enigmatic spirit in a rather morose if prophetic poem, written in 1927:

I do not know wherefrom
And not whereto
I stand in guilt
A strangeness barks around me
On all sides
Sparks what I do not want
Asks what I never knew
Oh! Even sunrays paint
Wet shadows in the sand
Unlike the shadows in my forever place
Out of the chimneys riddles foreign smoke
Behind the forest – heedless mountain goat –
Waits love for me perhaps
And children sing
My long forgotten name.[60]

The Ballets Russes

One of the most influential forces of artistic inspiration to arrive in early twentieth-century Britain was the Ballets Russes. With its staggeringly colourful costumes, stage sets and innovative music, nothing like it had ever been seen before, and young artists like Jessie King and Harry Clarke, both then living in Paris, were bowled over by its productions. Indeed they inspired a whole new generation of artists intent upon using its innovative and exotic colours, forms and atmospheres. Here for the first time was colour for colour's sake. Founded in Paris by Sergei Diaghilev in 1909, the Ballets Russes never performed in Russia but rather toured Europe, notably Paris and London, revolutionising modern theatre and dance until its demise in 1929. The original company included the notorious Vaslav Nijinsky and miraculous Anna Pavlova, who performed to the groundbreaking set designs and costumes of the period's most inventive artists, such as Leon Bakst, Alexandre Benois, Braque, Picasso, Ivan Bilibin and Maurice Utrillo. Music was specially composed by Stravinsky (*Petrushka*, 1911), Prokoviev, Ravel and Satie.

Diaghilev was a master of finding true talent. It is interesting that he had met Aubrey Beardsley in Dieppe in the summer of 1897, shortly before the artist's death, and was immediately won over by the young artist's talent. In 1898 he even commissioned an article about Beardsley for his cultural review *Mir Iskustva* (The World of Art), a publication which intended to liberate Russian art from its moribund past. In time Diaghilev influenced his costume designers like Bakst to adopt Beardsleyesque innovations on stage. Bakst was an established painter when he was taken up by Diaghilev in 1909, but, given a relatively free reign over costume and set design, he created miracles of colour and exoticism. His designs exhibited here for *Sheherazade* in 1910 and *Peri* in 1911 (see cats 134–135), as well as later creations for the more classical ballets *Sleeping Beauty* and *Cinderella* (1921) and *The Magic Flute* (1922) were breathtaking displays of colour and innovation, inspired largely by Russian folk art. He produced numerous sketches and, later, large finished

watercolours of his costume designs which were sold to an adoring audience. Such was the clamour for Bakst's influential designs that some of these were even reproduced as limited edition colour prints, like the *Peri* print shown here (cat. 135). When the young ceramics designer Daisy Makeig-Jones attended a 1911 production of the Ballets Russes at Covent Garden, she returned to her studio captivated by its breathtaking colours and intent upon using them – especially the oranges – for her elegant fantasy designs for Wedgwood. And, although Charles Ricketts decried the influence of the Ballets Russes upon his own stage designs, the latter do show a remarkable kinship to the spirit and vibrant colours of their productions.

ENCHANTMENT AT HOME

WITH NEWFOUND PROSPERITY came a growing demand for high quality decorative design and innovative objects to fill the large number of newly constructed homes of the nouveau riche. The so-called stockbroker belt, spawned by the railways, created a sprawling mock-Tudor suburbia which insidiously crept into the countryside and threatened its equilibrium. These were the tasteful trophy homes so beautifully described by John Galsworthy's *Forsyte Saga*. More to the critical point were the dreaded 'Cissy Villas', so wonderfully mocked by E. M. Forster in his classic novel *A Room with a View* (1908), which transformed the edges of towns and villages and introduced into country life a forced urban gentility complete with the newfangled bicycles and abhorrent motorcars sputtering down verdant country lanes which many found so appalling. Forster's model such family lived on a hillside at Windy Corner, 'as inevitable an ugliness as Nature's own creation', the house a mere uninspired box 'so commonplace, not to say impertinent' with a pretentious pseudo-Gothic turret constructed 'like a rhinoceros horn' onto the end of the building to allow the mistress to watch the daily flow of village traffic below her.

To help fill this new generation of rural snobs' demands for objects of appropriate tastefulness, the country's art schools sought to train young craftsmen and, more especially, craftswomen, to design the manufactured ceramics, tiles, furniture, wallpaper and fabrics of the future. Young middle-class women were favourites to be funnelled into the decorative arts programmes of the country's art schools, where they worked zealously and often anonymously for the manufacturers of quality home furnishings, like Liberty's in London, or such ceramic factories as Wedgwood, Coalport or Minton. The seeds of this design reform had been sown as early as the Great Exhibition of 1851, when its patron Prince Albert attempted to instil a national style of decoration upon the country's decorative arts to compete with continental pressures, particularly from his native Germany. As the century turned, the taste for dark, ecclesiastical High Victorian Gothic, with

its dark woods and heavy fabrics was transformed by the light-filled, highly painted interiors, simple-lined furniture and elegant fittings of the burgeoning Modern Age.

Daisy Makeig-Jones

One of the most extraordinary women of this decorative arts revival, and indeed a leading figure in the history of English ceramics, was Susannah Margaretta Makeig-Jones, known from childhood as Daisy. She and her colleagues represented the new generation of self-willed, ambitious English craftswomen who, like their Scottish contemporaries Jessie King, Annie French and Margaret Macdonald, abandoned the conventional role of the domesticated woman and left a legacy of enchanting, inventive and highly saleable works of decorative art. In the case of Makeig-Jones, this helped to propel English fantasy ceramics into the international marketplace.

She was born on 31 December 1881, the eldest daughter among seven children of a local doctor and his wife, the daughter of a solicitor, in a small Yorkshire village near Rotherham. From an early age she was a high spirited and adventurous child, who eventually turned her interests to drawing, training first with the local art master at Rugby School then, when the family moved to Devon, at the Torquay School of Art, with a brief three months in London at the Chelsea School of Art. She quickly displayed admirable application and the skills necessary to make a dedicated craftswoman. Fortunately her family knew the local Wedgwood pottery family and it was suggested that the ambitious young woman might try for a designer post there, which she gained in 1909, aged 28. She started on the factory floor – as was company policy – and cut a curious figure, the rather refined young woman surprising her working-class colleagues as she happily immersed herself in the dust and clay-filled workshops where she worked alongside them; but she was determined to understand the rudiments of ceramic production before she turned to design. In fact she stayed there on the shop floor for two years, before she joined the more genteel design studio as a trainee painter. There she immediately set to work upon her own series of designs for ceramic nurseryware, borrowing from favourite scenes in Hans Andersen's *Thumbelina* for inspiration.

With her forthright and highly opinionated nature, Makeig-Jones was a formidable woman who quickly rose to a position of responsibility. This was helped by the fact that she was soon related to the Wedgwoods by marriage – her brother had married a Wedgwood daughter. She would often go directly to the firm's board of trustees with her problems, circumventing her own bosses, which did not help relations with her colleagues. However it soon became apparent that she had a vision, one which the firm would recognize as a valuable asset, and in time she would help to save its ailing fortunes. At the dawn of the new century a pottery trade recession had hit the major factories in England and threatened the livelihoods of thousands. Makeig-Jones felt a new, exciting line of highly coloured 'china fancies' (bone china gift items), although designed for effect rather than utility, would appeal to the homes of the affluent if designed with a new, alluring exoticism. She turned for inspiration to her own childhood and her long love of fantasy and folk tales, especially the hugely popular series of Andrew Lang *Colour Fairy Books*, which had appeared during her childhood in 1889–1910, often filled with delightful Henry J. Ford illustrations. From each of these volumes Lang's message was a simple and appealing one to both children and their parents: he believed all children had 'an unblunted edge of belief and a fresh appetite for marvels' and these were the subjects and indeed the enchantment which Makeig-Jones was intent upon creating with Wedgwood's ceramics.[61]

The new ceramic line, which she called 'Fairyland Lustre', was a series of fine hand-painted bone china, eventually numbering over 100 separate designs. Each one was a meticulous and painstaking result of at least ten nerve-wracking steps, with glazes fired five to six times before the transferred design was hand-painted with metallic-based glazes and a final gold edging was applied. The intent was jewel-like intricacy and a rich, appealing visual surface which impelled the viewer's eye to pour over the minute clusters of fairies, the dense oriental-inspired landscapes and the exotic architecture which transformed Makeig-Jones's fairyland into a three-dimensional wonderland. Her first experiments in 1914 used simple, popular motifs borrowed from natural history – butterflies, dragons and hummingbirds – but by 1916 her imagination was in full flow and her love of fairies transformed into her signature vision. Indeed, she was so inspired by fantasy that she often proudly exclaimed, 'In Fairyland All Things Are Possible', which became her motto. It so inspired and fed her ambitions that she soon had over 62 separate Fairyland patterns in production. She was greatly influenced by contemporary illustrated books, especially the newly-published colour-plate fantasy gift books of Dulac and Rackham and above all Kay Nielsen's masterful *East of the Sun, West of the Moon* (1914). These colourful volumes contained a plethora of inspired and, for her purposes, extremely popular subject matter. Makeig-Jones brazenly borrowed from these masters and cleverly adopted elements from their

commercially winning formulas. Although she generally did not draw the designs for engraved transfers herself, she knew what would sell, and directed her team of designers accordingly.

A shrewd businesswoman, she served as Wedgwood's artistic director for over two decades, from 1916 to 1931, during which time her love of the business steered the foundering Wedgwood fortunes into more prosperous waters. She had long admired Chinese ceramics, especially the pale blue colour ('blue soufflé') which from 1912 she adopted into the now famous and lucrative Wedgwood 'Powder Blue' ware. But she also adored strong colours, especially orange, which she placed against dark, rich backgrounds for the ultimate striking effect. Like her contemporaries she had been dazzled by the colours and designs of Diaghilev's Ballets Russes, which she saw when they performed Stravinsky's *Petrushka* in 1911 at the Covent Garden Coronation Season: one admirer recalled how it 'burst like a vivid multi-coloured firework upon the muted colours that were then in fashion'.[62] It soon became apparent just how her true talent lay in selecting, combining and adapting such innovative elements for her discerning buying public. On close examination, Makeig-Jones's vision of Fairyland was a unique blend of sylvan beauty and a mesmeric devilishness, borrowed from the darker side: her battle scenes between fairies and tortured insects borrowed from that true early master Richard Doyle's *In Fairyland* (1870), while her own aggressive woodland elves are stretched across a metallic-tinged landscape in often hilarious and highly incongruous poses, such as the series with a fairy boxing match. Indeed potential purchasers were hard-pressed not to find among her 101 Fairyland patterns an appealing theme, such as the evocatively titled 'Black Fairyland', 'Dragon Lustre', 'Daylight Fairyland' or 'Garden of Paradise' – their names alone cleverly evoked a popular exoticism which helped to sell the numerous shapes and sizes of her fantastical ceramics (cats 138–141).

In time her Fairyland Lustreware became Wedgwood's bestselling line in ornamental bone china. Indeed, with this one line the firm was again able to compete successfully on the international stage with its 'High Class Fancy China' rivals Coalport, Crown Derby, Minton and Worcester. Sadly, by the time of the Art Deco-filled 1920s public tastes had changed yet again, in favour of a more simplistic, flat geometric line and a utilitarian approach to ceramics. Coupled with the Wall Street Crash in 1929, the fortunes of Wedgwood ceramics again waned. The firm cut Makeig-Jones's design list, cancelling 23 designs outright. By 1931 she was asked to retire; her personal aesthetic was by then believed to be no longer relevant or saleable for the Modern Age. At first she was outraged, and she chose to ignore the invitation. True to form, she was a fighter, and even when she finally relented and consented to leave Wedgwood that same year, she did so under a cloud of her own making. Her final statement indicated to the end she was still in control: she commanded her assistants to destroy all her newest design prototypes at that time. It was a sad, if not tawdry, end to a glorious career and, while the firm continued to produce some of

Makeig-Jones's lustreware designs until 1941, when the remaining stock was sold off in its entirety, she was out of the business. She retreated to Devon to care for her mother with her two sisters and there she died, on 1 July 1945, aged 63, leaving a legacy which is largely sustained today by the museums and a devoted band of collectors who willingly pay four- and five-figure sums for her delightfully unique ceramics.

THE LURE OF EXOTIC EMPIRE

ARTISTS WITH FINE ART AMBITIONS often had to turn to the decorative arts for sustenance, especially when popular tastes for their work changed and commissions dried up, or their once lucrative gallery paintings no longer sold. Versatility and resilience were invaluable traits for any ambitious twentieth-century artist, and indeed as the century progressed even established painters were forced to turn their hand to the fields of commercial illustration, poster design, or the design of decorative objects, ceramics, wallpapers, stained glass or furniture, which could help them maintain their careers in the arts throughout the century's various economic and aesthetic changes.

Sir Frank Brangwyn, RA

One such master of the versatile was the multi-talented painter Sir Frank Brangwyn. Born into High Victorian Britain, Brangwyn successfully painted and designed his way well into the Modern Age; at his death in 1957, he was a much-lauded artistic giant of the British art scene and, marking his success among the establishment, he had been created a knight of the realm. Brangwyn was born in 1867, the son of a Welsh architect. He was largely self-taught, but with his quick eye and seemingly indefatigable energies he recognised how the study of the decorative arts could help pave the way for a more exalted career as a gallery artist. He had watched the rise of the Arts and Crafts Movement, with its innovative yet spare decorative, hand-crafted furnishings for the late nineteenth-century home, and even began work for its prestigious and highly influential pioneer, William Morris's Oxford Street workshops in London, where he was first employed as a copyist of Flemish tapestries. This led to more prestigious work, including carpet and stained glass designs for Samuel Bing's famous Art Nouveau emporium, L'Art Nouveau in Paris. Later he worked on ceramic designs for the firms of Royal Doulton and the popular earthenware of A. J. Wilkinson's. As an inveterate and lifelong traveller, Brangwyn soon set off to the continent, and over the years he used his many sea journeys and travels to inspire the numerous nautical oils and watercolours he successfully exhibited in the London galleries: he first showed at the Royal Academy in 1885, aged just eighteen, and was made a full member in 1919.

In time Brangwyn's subjects became more exotic, as he explored the warmer climes of Spain, Italy and northern Africa in search of new colourful subjects. Although not generally known for his illustrations, he illustrated about 40 volumes and created over 70 bookplate designs, in which he concentrated largely upon classical or contemporary themes. But he loved foreign themes, and even at an early age he produced a series of illustrations to a new edition of *The Arabian Nights* which was published in 1897, followed by the beloved Spanish classic, Cervantes's *Don Quixote*, in 1898. He even provided 20 oil-painted illustrations, 'explosive in colour', which were reproduced in a new edition of *The Rubaiyat of Omar Khayyam* in 1919. Mostly, however, his colourful themes were painted or etched, drawn for carpets or murals, or even inserted upon his furniture designs, as in his marvellous wooden print chest shown here (cat. 144).

Brangwyn loved what might be termed 'The Cult of the Exotic', and he became a favourite advocate of the diversity of the far-flung reaches of the British Empire. As a staunch supporter of the Empire, he was a natural choice to be commissioned by the British government to design and engineer one of the many elaborate public spectacles to promote the economic influence of the Empire at the British Empire Exhibition of 1924–25. This exhibition was a remarkable feat of public relations, held in and around the newly-built Empire Stadium (later renamed Wembley Stadium) in north-west London, ten years after the start of World War One. Its predecessor was the hugely influential Franco-British Exhibition of 1908, set in its own purpose-built grounds at White City, London. Allied with French colonial flare, this early extravaganza had set the standards for a new philosophy of national unity ('when British solidarity is adorned by French grace, a combination is reached which embraces the highest achievements of the human race'). The British Empire Exhibition hoped to play upon its successful predecessor and was given full royal credence when it was opened by King George V. He spoke for the first time via a series of 'wireless amplifiers' to an estimated audience of five million listeners. His speech was a clarion call for cooperation and understanding throughout a war-torn Empire and the exhibition was heralded as a 'vast graphic illustration of the spirit of free and tolerant cooperation' which, 'if the Exhibition led to an expansion of the Empire trade', he hoped would 'at the same time assist the economic life of the world disorganized by the war'. To force home his point, there were breathtaking displays of local products from the colonies, within their own specially-designed theme pavilions. Much like the earlier Franco-British Exhibition, with its colonial 'villages' of imported colonial products and peoples, the British Empire Exhibition was truly a World's Fair for the British and was thrillingly filled with the most exhilarating, unusual and remarkable exotica from as far afield as

India (although at one stage the exhibition's success was marred by an attempted Indian boycott), Burma, Fiji, the Gold Coast and Bermuda, whose pavilion was designed as a large Caribbean villa; there was even a replica of the Old London Bridge, as well as a huge Canadian pavilion set against a painted background of the Rocky Mountains, and an Australian building stuffed with native foods. Crowds flocked to experience the excitement and marvel at the many products available throughout the Empire. Some of the country's best artists, like C. R. Nevinson, were commissioned to design alluring posters for the trains and the Underground, which promised to willing visitors 'Music Wherever You Go', 'Treasures From Overseas' or urged them to 'Make Up A Party', and assured all war-weary visitors 'Come to Wembley And Be Happy.'[63]

When Brangwyn was approached to design one of the many spectacles planned to present the various countries to their public, he devised a grandiose vision of colonial life in which the entire stadium was to be transformed, like one of the classical games in the Roman Forum, 'into an exotic landscape comprising elements from all parts of the Empire'. Against an incongruous background of the Canadian Rockies which loomed unfortunately over the stadium, he planned a roofed structure to look like it was supported only by the trees of the jungle. More shockingly to the organisers, he demanded the entire stadium be flooded like a huge lake, upon which he planned to float a full-sized sailing ship. He also wanted all the dominions and colonies to 'send parades of natives in national costume accompanied by exotic animals', but this was quickly rejected by parsimonious officials who feebly assured Brangwyn there was no need to import battalions of natives as 'arrangements had been made to hire a few dozen theatrical costumes'.[64]

Following this unpleasant brush with officialdom, Brangwyn became thoroughly aware of just how difficult public commissions, especially government ones, could be. Yet the lesson was not entirely learned, although perhaps it should have been. He was next approached and greatly flattered by an even more prestigious team of government officials, who suggested he might be the perfect man to design a new mural for the Houses of Parliament. This seemed the ultimate artist commission, to have one's creation immortalised in the country's most important public building. Sadly this ill-fated project was destined to become the most complicated, controversial and eventually soul-destroying public commission of his career. Nevertheless, partly for the prestige and the patriotic nature of the work, Brangwyn agreed to the project, not knowing that it would totally tax his energies and his strength for seven years and then languish unappreciated and unused. It was to be his masterpiece, a work inspired yet again by the Empire and his own vision of what its many peoples and habitats should look like. He was immensely impressed by the magnitude and importance of the commission's plan: in 1924 the House of Lords wanted to complete the Victorian mural scheme started by Daniel Maclise under Prince Albert, and to commemorate the end of World War One they proposed a huge mural covering the enormous expanse of 3,000

Fig. 20: Detail of Brangwyn's Empire Panels (see cats 142–143).

square feet of the prestigious Royal Gallery. It was hoped whoever designed the mural would enhance the interior of the most powerful government building in Britain, and instil a nationalist sentiment which, after ten years of war, would inspire all who saw it.

Brangwyn was proposed by Lord Iveagh, who felt since he was a veteran war artist and much-lauded muralist he was the perfect candidate; he even agreed to pay the £20,000 fee. For his part, Brangwyn was immediately flattered by the scale and grandeur of the project and he approached the commission with characteristic fervour; it was after all a true mark of honour to be chosen and he vowed to the press that he would rise to the challenge. A strong patriot, he declared his aims from the start were based upon 'the men whom the panels would commemorate [who] had died to save Britain and the Empire and so it seemed natural to portray the people, the flowers, the fruits and the fauna of the far-flung territories of the British dominion'. He then concluded rather pompously, 'My theme is the Empire, in all its majesty and multitudinous resource, for that, as I see it, is the most fitting commemoration of the things for which we fought.' His design scheme was to be ' a continuous pageant, a symbolic record of the unity and fertility, the health and abundance of the Empire.' With no geographical logic intended, each of the panels would eventually show an insular world of beauty and plenitude, a fantasy which was firmly based upon Brangwyn's very personal idea of the exotic.[65]

The genesis of these enormous panels is a fascinating look at the period's love of the exotic, which would dominate the decorative arts well into the middle of the twentieth century. Indeed it could be said that Brangwyn was largely following the tenets of a new and exciting popular taste for all things exotic, as he devised his own mural kingdom. He determined to use all things colourful and ethnic to force home his ideal. He zealously prepared drawings from life, filled his garden with tropical plants, visited the London Zoo to draw the foreign animals, used his wife's beloved parrot, and even commandeered a pet goat and dog for his designs. Models proved difficult, but gradually word got out that he needed Caribbean characters, and they soon appeared at his studio door unannounced, which delighted him: 'One, a woman, is a professional wrestler,' he exclaimed to the *Sunday Express*; another, 'a large, massive Negress' arrived in a totally unsuitable full evening dress with her three young sons dressed in equally inappropriate velvet, wearing Eton collars, but in time he convinced them all to pose in the nude as he felt all true natives should be depicted. He also found inspiration in the colourful, elaborately patterned tiles of Moorish architecture, in the intricacies of early French tapestries, and the Balinese flat decorative patterns which he used for the foliage designs surrounding his figures. Indeed each themed panel was the result of hundreds of sketches and drawings (cat. 143). He worked diligently until 1930, when the Royal Fine Arts commission insisted upon seeing the five finished panels in situ. Brangwyn reluctantly agreed, and in the end this proved a fatal mistake: all five panels were carefully studied, deemed inappropriate and declined outright by the commissioners (fig. 20).

According to his biographer, the finished panels 'have a sort of primitive quality which makes them loud and almost ostentatious. They are utterly flat, so wholly two-dimensional, that they appear to be devoid of tonal contrast. They are luxuriant and commanding. Plants, animals and figures stand shoulder upon shoulder filling out every inch of canvas. In a triumph of attitudes the abundance and fecundity of nature is expressed.'[66] So convinced was Brangwyn of the validity of his decorative scheme that he adopted it for a series of rug designs for the firm of James Templeton. Sadly, public opinion differed, and more importantly his official employers felt cheated. They declared his scheme frivolous, flamboyant and inappropriate to the sanctity of a government chamber, his oriental processions and scenery 'indicate no connection with the Empire as such; nor does the subject-matter or its treatment suggest any degree of relation to Imperial or Dominion Parliaments'. Art critics weighed in with contrasting opinions; the *Illustrated London News* hailed the murals as 'the most splendid unit of decorative painting in Europe since Tintoretto ceased his work in the Doges Palace in Venice'; others, like the much respected musician and pillar of the establishment Sir John Barbirolli, dismissed the panels simply as 'all tits and bananas'.[67]

In the end the panels were never hung, and languished unseen. This left Brangwyn devastated. It was only in 1933 that they were given a special display airing at the Daily Mail Ideal Home Exhibition, and the following year, after structural repairs were completed, they were presented, along with numbers of studies and sketches to the newly-named Brangwyn Hall in Swansea (now a concert and arts centre), where they remain today. In 1935 a series of commemorative ceramic plaques based upon Brangwyn's

subjects were issued, painted by the famed Art Deco ceramicist Clarice Cliff, but these remain mere shadows of the grand original decorative scheme (cat. 142). Moreover, the public rejection of his masterpiece left Brangwyn angry and embittered; in particular he abhorred what he considered his unfair treatment by the popular press, which he earnestly believed had been given the fatal power to damn his creation. He instigated his own campaign of vilification and lashed out at the growing power of the press to praise or damn artistic ventures, which gave their creators little or no redress. Moreover, he attacked the rise of what he called 'the cult of the artist', which he saw as fuelled by the attention-seeking art world, with its grubby battery of agents and publicists intent upon promoting even the feeblest of artistic efforts. As a card-carrying member of the establishment, he dismissed Modern Art as mere 'street art', which he saw as 'the produce of an undisciplined mob of competent individuals working only to attract attention'. Money, power and celebrity seemed to drive the new-generation artist – as indeed it does today – and the perspicacious Brangwyn wanted no part of it. When he died in 1956, he was eulogised as the period's most distinguished professional artist, who had been duly knighted by the Queen and honoured internationally. But Sir Frank Brangwyn, RA was soon to be relegated to the second tier of British artists and today he remains an acknowledged but largely uninspired figure. His designs and works of decorative art are perhaps more interesting to the Modern Age than his multitudes of large, overpainted oil paintings, dull landscape watercolours, drawings and prints.

With Brangwyn's death, and indeed the demise of his generation of Golden Age artists and illustrators – especially those who had survived into the middle of the twentieth century – it seemed to many that standards of fine artistic production had taken a further slide downwards towards the superficial, the ephemeral and the downright bad. In tracing the lives and careers of the 'Age of Enchantment' artists in this exhibition, it soon becomes apparent just how dependent they were upon the vagaries of popular taste, and the ephemeral nature of their art. Indeed commercial illustration was always linked to a fluctuating economy and with it a fickle popular taste. But the demise of the perfectionist standards of such well-trained giants as the Detmolds, Sidney Sime, Edmund Dulac and Kay Nielsen, who in the end lived out their careers in disappointment, anger and soul-destroying neglect, is a sad end to the story of such a glorious period in British decorative art. As they watched the century progress and its poor standards of artistic taste surround them, it was for many too much to bear. Some died alone, embittered and lost as well as forgotten, like Sime and Dulac, despite having enjoyed unimaginable fame (and, in Dulac's case, fortune) in their heydays. Moreover, it is equally disheartening that today's artists are no longer trained to draw and paint after their masters, and indeed craftsmen no longer study history or – as the Age of Enchantment artists did – turn to the Near or Far East for inspiration. In short, today the lessons of the past languish. The Golden Age of Illustration inspired a standard of perfectionism, as is clearly borne out in the well-conceived and immaculately crafted objects, as well as the wonderfully detailed and inspired illustrations exhibited here. In our present world of shoddiness and surface, such devotion to craftsmanship above all else is a concept which seems very alien indeed. And yet our ability to appreciate fully the wonder of the objects in 'The Age of Enchantment' must be linked to this outmoded concept of perfectionism. Kay Nielsen's proud claim – made at the sad end of his long life – that he spent his entire career 'devoted to the lyrical and the poetic' seems to too many of us today, in our jaded world of speed and false economies, a rather feeble and misguided artistic ambition. Hopefully things will change.

NOTES

1. See Walter Crane, *Of the Decorative Illustration of Books Old and New*, 1901

2. Julius Meier-Graefe, *Entwicklungs geschichte der moderne Kunst II*, 1904, p. 603; see also Linda Zatlin, *Beardsley, Japanisme and the Perversion of the Victorian Ideal*, Cambridge, 1997

3. *The Idler*, March 1897, p. 200

4. *The Idler*, March 1897, p. 201

5. Quoted in Stanley Weintraub, *Beardsley*, 1967, pp. 42–43

6. Robert Ross, *Aubrey Beardsley*, 1909, p. 39

7. Quoted in Weintraub, op.cit., p.113

8. Introduction to Aubrey Beardsley's *Under the Hill*, 1904 edition, pp. viii–ix

9. *The Idler*, 1898, p. 544

10. *Under the Hill*, op. cit., p. ix

11. *The Pall Mall Gazette*, 2 November 1904

12. Quoted in Weintraub, op. cit., p. 246

13. See Max Nordau, *Degeneration*, 1895, English edition, quoted by Matthew Sturgis in *Passionate Attitudes*, 1995, p. 235

14. Oscar Wilde to Laurence Housman, 14 December [1898], in Rupert Hart Davis, *Letters of Oscar Wilde*, 1962, p. 771

15. Laurence Housman, *The Unexpected Years*, 1937, p. 113

16. Laurence Housman, *Arthur Boyd Houghton*, 1896, p. 22

17. Leonee and Richard Ormand, *Lord Leighton*, 1975, pp. 117–18

18. Hart Davis, op. cit., p. 713

19. Charles Kaines Jackson, *The Booklover's Magazine*, May 1908, p. 235

20. Obituaries in *The Times* and *The Manchester Guardian*, 21 February 1959

21. J. G. P. Delaney, *Charles Ricketts*, 1990, pp. 46–47

22. Quoted in Stephen Calloway, *Charles Ricketts*, 1979, p. 16

23. Ibid, p. 24

24. See Simon Heneage and Henry Ford, *Sidney Sime*, 1980

25. Haldane Macfall in *St Paul's Magazine*, September 1899, also *Strand Magazine*, October 1908

26. Heneage and Ford, op. cit., p. 23

27. See the article 'Minor Magus' [Arthur Machan] in *The New Yorker*, 6 December 2004, p. 115

28. Nicola Gordon Bowe, *Harry Clarke*, 1989, pp. 1, 7

29. *The Studio*, Special Winter Number 1923; also *The Irish Times*, November 1925

30. *The Irish Statesman*, 13 December 1919

31. Harry Clarke to T. Bodkin, 2 November 1925, quoted in Gordon Bowe, op. cit., p. 191

32. *The New Republic*, July 1894, pp. 53–54

33. Beatrix Potter's diary entry was for 17 November 1896; see Leslie Linder (ed.), *The Journal of Beatrix Potter*, London, 1986

34. E. A. Taylor in *The Booklover's Magazine for 1904* (reprinted by IBIS, London, 2005)

35. See Rodney Engen, *Arthur Rackham*, Dulwich Picture Gallery exhibition catalogue, London, 2002

36. See Christie's (London) Book Department auction catalogue, 15 December 1993, Lot 121

37. Quoted by James Hamilton in *Arthur Rackham*, 1995, p. 72

38. C. S. Lewis, *Surprised by Joy*, 1955, p. 74

39. Autograph letter, Barbara Soper to Derek Hudson, Victoria and Albert Museum, quoted in Rodney Engen, *Arthur Rackham*, op. cit., p. 12

40. Quoted in Leo de Freitas, *Charles Robinson*, 1976, p. 10

41. *The Studio*, V, 1895, p. 146

42. *The Bookman*, II, New York, 1896

43. De Freitas, op. cit., p. 14; quoted in Mary Clive, *The Day of Reckoning*, 1967, p. 87

44. William Heath Robinson, *My Line of Life*, 1938

45. Unpublished manuscript biography by Ian MacPhail. I am grateful to this enthusiastic author for his generous sharing of his Detmold research.

46. See the article by Campbell Dodgson, *Print Collector's Quarterly*, December 1922, pp. 373–405

47. Dodgson, op. cit., p. 384

48. MacPhail manuscript, op. cit., p. 10

49. Nicholas Alfrey and Richard Verdi, *The Detmolds*, 1983, p. 6

50. See Diana Johnson in *Fantastic Illustration and Design in Britain 1850–1930*, 1979, p. 80

51. See Alastair Duncan, *Art Deco*, 1988

52. Quoted by Anne Hughey, *Edmund Dulac: His Book Illustrations*, 1995, introduction

53. Colin White, *Edmund Dulac*, 1976, pp. 28–29

54. Ibid, pp. 64–65

55. Ibid, p. 194

56. Hildegarde Flanner, 'Memoir' in *The Unknown Paintings of Kay Nielsen*, 1977, p. 2

57. Keith Nicholson, *Kay Nielsen*, 1975, p. 3

58. Ibid, p. 5

59. Nielsen's unpublished original nineteen (of 20) gouaches to *The Thousand and One Nights* are now in the Los Angeles County Museum and reproduced in *The Unknown Paintings of Kay Nielsen*, 1977.

60. For a full illustrated account of Alastair's remarkable achievements see Victor Arwas, *Alastair*, London, 1979, from which this was quoted.

61. See Una des Fontaines in *Miss Jones and her Fairyland*, Victoria and Albert Museum catalogue, 1990

62. Ibid, p. 13

63. Rodney Brangwyn, *Brangwyn*, 1978, p. 216

64. Ibid, p. 217

65. Ibid, pp. 238–39

66. Ibid, p. 259

67. Paul Liss, *Frank Brangwyn*, Fine Art Society catalogue, 2006, p. 36

Catalogue

The Age of Enchantment
Fantasy in Britain 1890—1930

THE LURE OF THE FAR EAST

With the mid-nineteenth century's opening of Western trade with Japan and China, a flood of Asian products and art works poured into Britain and inspired numerous artists and decorative designers. The Arts and Crafts Movement of the 1870s embraced this exciting oriental aesthetic with its spare, elegant simplicity, as did the period's book illustrators like Walter Crane, who had discovered by chance how Japanese prints — then used as wrapping paper for imported porcelain — held the key to a refreshing new approach to creating space in illustration. Artists like the painter James McNeill Whistler, the architect-designer E. W. Godwin and of course Aubrey Beardsley were captivated by this uniquely Eastern approach to design.

1 A Group of Western Sailors Dressed as Japanese, c.1900

Sepia-toned photograph by C. Enami,
Yokohama, Japan
13 x 9 cm
Private Collection

Western trade with Japan began in 1853, and
with it came the vogue for all things Japanese,
which in turn exerted a tremendous influence
upon British designers and artists and their
public, the fashion-conscious middle-class
households that were filled with imitation
oriental ceramics and furniture, and illustrations
produced in the Japanese manner. Photographs
such as this were taken in Japan, to be sent
home as mementos of the West's new
fascination with the oriental way of life.

2 Wood screen, late nineteenth century

Mahogany and brass
160 x 192 cm
Private Collection

Such screens were very popular with the
burgeoning middle classes, and were hung with
pictures or William Morris fabrics – here his
'Seaweed' pattern, in the Aesthetic manner. They
were typical of the late nineteenth century's
vogue for clean oriental line and suggestive of
the rice paper screens used to divide the rooms
of Japanese houses.

THE AESTHETE'S PEACOCK

The peacock was a late nineteenth-century talisman, a symbol of decadence and rarefied aesthetics borne out of this remarkable bird's history. The tyrannical King Herod was famous for his peacock menagerie and even offered Salome 100 white peacocks for her seductive dance; biblically the peacock represented immortality, while in Russian folklore it claimed a phoenix-like reverence. By the nineteenth century, the bird's brilliant feathers and quixotic attitude inspired the period's finest artists: Dante Gabriel Rossetti kept peacocks in his Cheyne Walk garden in the 1860s, E. W. Godwin designed a peacock wallpaper, and the painter James McNeill Whistler created his famous Peacock Room (fig. 1) for his patron Frederick Leyland in 1876, while Whistler also inspired Oscar Wilde to embed peacock feathers into his Tite Street drawing room ceiling. By the 1890s the bird had become an Art Nouveau icon, especially after the influential Aubrey Beardsley found the peacock a perfect foil for his fantasies and incorporated it into his early book illustrations for *Le Morte Darthur* and in his most famous drawings to *Salome*. Later their artistic disciples would develop these peacock themes and the vogue for the Art Nouveau peacock filled the homes of the aspiring middle classes.

3 A pair of Chinese peacock-design curtains, late nineteenth century

Velvet, gold, silver and coloured metallic thread
300 x 119 cm
Private Collection

These splendid curtains were produced in China for the late nineteenth-century English decorative market. Such works would have graced the sumptuous drawing rooms of the wealthy aesthetes.

4 AUBREY BEARDSLEY
'The Peacock Skirt', 1894

Line block proof on Japanese vellum
22.5 x 16 cm
Collection of Dr Michael Richard Barclay

Designed for Oscar Wilde's *Salome* (1894), this remains one of Beardsley's most popular inventions and incorporates the peacock's elaborate feather motif into Salome's cloak. Beardsley's mastery of the peacock as a design element was legendary, as were all his illustrations for the book.

5 KAY NIELSEN

'She stopped to speak to him; then, altering her mind, went on her way',
1912

Watercolour, pen and ink, heightened
with gold, signed and dated 1912
31.5 x 28 cm
Kendra and Allan Daniel Collection

This peacock-inspired fantasy borrowed
heavily from Beardsley's *Salome*
illustration 'The Peacock Skirt' (cat. 4),
and illustrated the chapter 'The Dancing
Princesses' in the Danish illustrator Kay
Nielsen's first successful book *In Powder
and Crinoline* (1912).

6 EDWARD and MAURICE DETMOLD

'Peacocks', 1897

Watercolour, pencil and bodycolour on
tinted paper, signed and dated
18 x 11.5 cm
Private Collection

This sensitive rendering of peacocks in a
landscape was created jointly by the child
prodigies the Detmold twins, who made
their reputations by creating collaborative
animal etchings, including some of the
finest and most spirited peacock prints
ever produced. Remarkably this
watercolour was painted when the twins
were just thirteen years of age.

THE AGE OF DECADENCE

By the 1880s and 1890s, innovative artists and writers embraced the philosophy of decadence and were particularly inspired by the shadowy pleasures and moral temptations associated with life in France. The French author Huysmans's pioneering *A Rebours* (Against Nature) encapsulated this new religious yearning for hedonistic pleasure and Oscar Wilde became the High Priest of Decadence, his preface to *The Picture of Dorian Gray* claiming, 'There is no such thing as a moral or immoral book. Books are well written or badly written.' His artistic acolyte was the young Aubrey Beardsley who, with schoolboyish glee, revelled in shocking and challenging what he believed to be the staid and hypocritical world around him.

Aubrey Beardsley (1872–1898)

7 FREDERICK H. EVANS
Aubrey Beardsley, 1894

Photogravure after the 'private portrait study' platinum photograph by Frederick H. Evans, printed signature in the plate
Swan Electric Engraving Company, 1895
13 x 10 cm
Private Collection

Frederick H. Evans (1853–1943) was a bookseller and publisher who turned to photography in the 1880s. By 1900 he had created some of the most telling and remarkable photographic portraits of literary personalities of the age. His style was to concentrate upon the face, with little detail. Beardsley was delighted with this image, writing to Evans on 20 August 1894, 'I think the photos are splendid, couldn't be better.' It remains the most famous portrait of the young artist, who died four years later.

From a private portrait study by Frederick H. Evans.

Swan Electric Engraving Co.

8 Aubrey Beardsley at Mentone

Photogravure after the photograph by
Monsigneur Abel, Mentone
Published by Leonard Smithers and Co., 1899
11.3 x 13.5 cm
Private Collection

Towards the end of his life, Beardsley escaped
London and took up residence in Menton (or
Mentone as he called it, in deference to its Italian
past) for his health. There he worked upon his
promised *Volpone* and *Mademoiselle de Maupin*
illustrations in between bouts of tubercular illness.
He died in this room, surrounded by his beloved
Mantegna engravings and his two favourite
candlesticks on 16 March 1898, aged just 25.

10 Design for the front cover of *The Yellow Book*, Vol.1, April 1894

Proof line block engraving
20.5 x 15.5 cm
Private Collection

As the magazine's artistic director, Beardsley created four cover designs for *The Yellow Book*, printed in black on yellow cloth boards, which made them especially eye-catching. The Beardsley scholar Brian Reade likened this bold, innovative composition, with its exaggerated lady's hat cut out, and the hard, flat, jagged treatment of the dotted gown, to the French style Pointillism or the spatter on Lautrec's posters. To Reade the whole daring composition was a wonderful prefiguration of the modern age, with 'the seeds of Cubism and of many kinds of abstract art'.

9 Drawing Table used by Aubrey Beardsley

Wood, painted black, with engraved brass plaque lettered 'Aubrey Beardsley's Work Table rescued by R. A. Walker *c*.1920'
73 x 118 x 82.5 cm
Provenance: Aubrey Beardsley 1894–95; Robert Armitage Walker, *c*.1920; Anthony Walker, by descent; then present owner, purchased 2001
Stephen Calloway

This simple table formed part of the aesthetic furnishings of Beardsley's house at 114 Cambridge Street, Pimlico, which he shared with his actress sister Mabel. It was the table on which he drew his famous *Salome* illustrations. Flushed with the success of *The Yellow Book*, which he then art edited, he had moved into a four-storey, stucco-fronted house in 1894, which he decorated with an aesthete's flair, roping in his friend Aymer Vallance and his sister to help. On the first floor were two connecting rooms used as a drawing room-cum-studio, with black-painted furniture, woodwork and floors, and orange walls (orange being the colour of decadence, according to his mentor Huysmans). Light from the tall windows was curtailed by thick dark curtains 'designed in France', with chairs covered in blue- and white-striped fabric for contrast. Beardsley favoured a tall wicker armchair with padded wings at its top, which he set before this Regency worktable. The walls were hung sparsely with a few of his originals and Japanese prints. Visitors described the room's overall effect as 'sombre' or 'dark or severe, almost frigid'. Following the arrest of Oscar Wilde and Beardsley's dismissal from *The Yellow Book* by John Lane in 1895, he was forced to leave this house. Later this table was rescued from the abandoned house by Robert Armitage Walker, who bought various items and attached the explanatory brass plaque to the table.

11a-b Two full-page illustrations
to *Le Morte Darthur*, 1893–94

Line block
each 21 x 16.5 cm
Private Collection

11a 'How Four Queens Found Launcelot Sleeping'

Full-page illustration for Chapter V, Book VI
of *Le Morte Darthur*

Beardsley completed over 300 pen and ink designs for
Dent's edition of Malory's *Le Morte Darthur*. It was his
first book illustration commission. He willingly adopted
a medieval format and borders emulating the popular
productions of William Morris's Kelmscott Press, while
the figures were borrowed from Burne-Jones, his early
champion. However, he imbued a special boldness of
design in each of the full-page illustrations or decorated
texts and brought his own brand of medievalism to the
head- and tail-pieces which make his edition of the
classic tale a unique work. Nevertheless William Morris
was outraged by what he saw as blatant plagiarism,
while Beardsley dismissed this criticism as absurd.

11b 'Sir Launcelot and the Witch Hellawes'

Full-page illustration for Chapter XV, Book VI
of *Le Morte Darthur*

12 **'Salome and Jokanaan'** from *Salome*, 1894

Proof line block on Japanese vellum
21.2 x 11.2 cm
Collection of Dr Michael Richard Barclay

Beardsley's *Salome* drawings set new standards for
decadent-themed draughtsmanship and inspired a
new generation of young artist-illustrators intent
upon emulating his distinctive style. This version
was first published in *The Studio* magazine.

13 **Design for the frontispiece to *Plays* by John Davidson, 1894**

Pen and Indian ink over pencil
28.6 x 18.7 cm
Tate. Bequeathed by John Lane 1926

The people represented here are said to be (from left to right): Mabel Beardsley, the artist's sister; Henry Harland (then literary editor of *The Yellow Book*) as a faun; Oscar Wilde as Bacchus with legs bound; Sir Augustus Harris, manager of Covent Garden, Drury Lane and Her Majesty's Theatre; Richard Le Gallienne, man-of-letters; and the dancer Adeline Genée. Speculation has centred around the Wildean figure – that Mabel Beardsley, Aubrey's sister, may be showing some interest in the obviously unavailable (hence bound) Oscar Wilde – and that Beardsley himself is the faun figure. The almost abstract landscape background was remarkable for the period.

14 **'Venus between Terminal Gods', 1895**

Design for *The Story of Venus and Tannhauser*
Pen and Indian ink touched with white
22.5 x 17.8 cm
Trustees of The Cecil Higgins Art Gallery, Bedford

This design for the frontispiece of Beardsley's
romantic novel was much admired by Sir Frederic
Leighton and others. Critics have suggested
Beardsley borrowed from Laurence Housman's
background interlace in his frontispiece to *The
End of Elfintown* (1894).

15 **'The Abbe', 1896**

Pen and Indian ink
25 x 17.5 cm
Victoria and Albert Museum

This drawing to illustrate Beardsley's unfinished novel *Under
the Hill* appeared in *The Savoy*, No. 1, January 1896. Originally
named 'The Abbe Aubrey', this portrait was drawn by
Beardsley to represent the heady lines of a true aesthete: 'The
place where he stood waved drowsily with strange flowers,
heavy with perfume, dripping with odours. Gloomy and
nameless weeds not to be found in Mentzelius. Huge moths,
so richly winged they must have banqueted upon tapestries
and royal stuffs, slept on the pillars that flanked either side of
the gateway, the eyes of all the moths remained open and
were burning and bursting with a mesh of veins.'

16 **'The Battle of the Beaux and the Belles', 1896**

Illustration for
The Rape of the Lock
Pen and Indian ink
25.7 x 17.6 cm
The Trustees of The Henry
Barber Trust, The University
of Birmingham

This *tour de force* of pen work, with its dense stippling in emulation of eighteenth-century engravers like Bartolozzi, was also a masterful pastiche, adapted from Beardsley's study of historical costumes: the men's clothes are appropriate to the poem (1712–14), while the women's costumes are based upon styles in vogue during the 1780s. The rococo chair is inspired by designs of the mid-eighteenth century. Beardsley's nine drawings to Pope's *Rape of the Lock* were the most admired of his works immediately after his untimely death in 1898.

17 Proof initial 'V' from *Volpone*, 1898

Line block on Japanese vellum
18 x 16 cm
Collection of Dr Michael Richard Barclay

This ingenious classically-inspired initial, one of just four designs plus frontispiece for *Volpone* which Beardsley completed before his death, was owned by Beardsley's publisher Leonard Smithers. Beardsley excitedly worked upon *Volpone* while in self-imposed exile in Menton, and found Ben Jonson's delightful satire on greed and lust most inspiring: Volpone was 'a splendid sinner, [who] compels our admiration by the fineness and very excess of his wickedness. We are scarcely shocked by his lust, so magnificent is the vehemence of his passion, and we marvel and are aghast rather than disgusted at his cunning and audacity.' The book was issued posthumously.

18 'The Lady with the Monkey', *c*.1897

Illustration to Theophile Gautier's
Mademoiselle de Maupin
Pen and Indian ink and wash
20 x 16.9 cm
Victoria and Albert Museum

This late drawing was originally intended for Beardsley's edition of *Volpone*, but was eventually published as the last plate to the posthumous volume, *Six Drawings illustrating Theophile Gautier's Romance Mademoiselle de Maupin by Aubrey Beardsley*, published by Leonard Smithers in London in 1898.

EXQUISITE AND PRECIOUS TALES

With the aesthetes came the vogue for the exquisite book as object: fine bindings and tasteful typography characterised these volumes, which were published in strictly limited numbers to appeal to a rarefied book-collecting market. Bound in vellum or fine cloth with gilt interlace, strapwork and lettering, and filled with a careful selection of wood-engraved illustrations, initials and head- and tail-pieces often modelled after Italian Renaissance models, each was a masterwork of the bookmaker's art never before seen in Britain. Poetry, precious prose poems and self-indulgent essays received this treatment, most notably published by either John Lane or Charles Ricketts at The Vale Press. The master of these rarefied volumes was undoubtedly Laurence Housman, the illustrator, poet and creator of exquisite tales, who insisted upon the finest printing and production for all of his work.

Laurence Housman (1865–1959)

19 W. H. CAFFYN
Laurence Housman

Pen and Indian ink on card
11.8 x 9 cm
Private Collection

There are few drawings of Housman, although there are numerous photographs and even a portrait bust in the National Portrait Gallery. His distinctive goatee beard and thick silvery hair were easily picked out of a crowd. He in fact depicted himself as a cowled St Francis in the frontispiece to his edition of *The Little Flowers of St Francis* (1898).

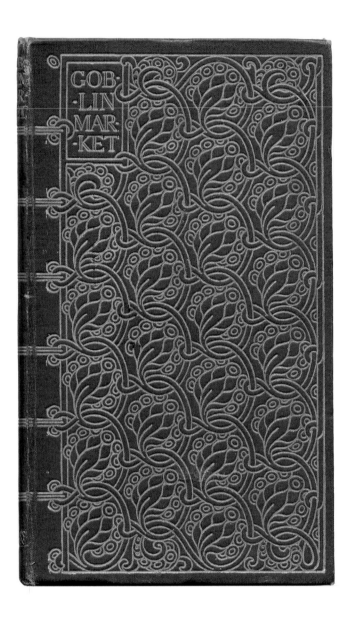

20 Binding design by Housman for
Goblin Market **by Christina Rossetti**

London: Macmillan and Company, 1893
Private Collection

This pivotal book design of the late nineteenth century helped to launch Housman's career as a book designer and illustrator. His 43 wood-engraved illustrations, engraved by his sister Clemence, were critically praised and helped Housman secure the patronage of Sir Frederic Leighton.

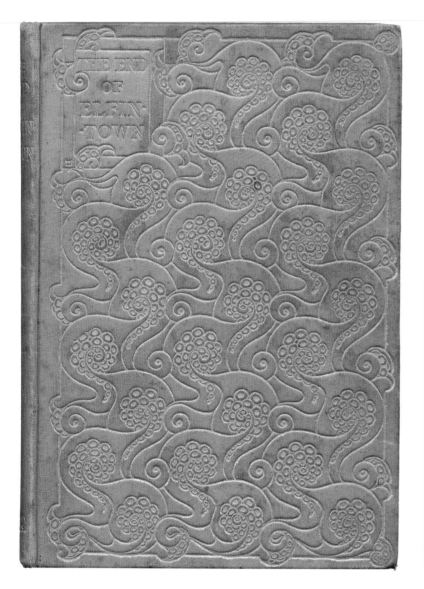

21 **Binding design by Housman for**
The End of Elphintown **by Jane Barlow**

London: Macmillan and Company, 1894
Private Collection

Housman's early bindings were *tours de force*
of elegance and invention, and he supervised
every element of their production from the
choice of cloth to the gilt decoration.

22 **Title-page design for** *The House of Joy*, **1895**

Pen and Indian ink, initialled
22 x 15 cm
Victoria and Albert Museum

Housman wrote the eight fairy tales in this, the first of three
illustrated compilations of his stories and tales, published by
Kegan Paul throughout the 1890s. His design here borrowed
heavily from medieval manuscripts with heavy ornamental
borders framing each delicate conception, a clear homage to
his colleagues William Morris and Charles Ricketts. The
original drawing was created larger and photographically
reduced to fit the published border.

23 **'The Invisible Princess'**, 1897

Pen and black ink with touches of
brown ink and bodycolour, initialled
19.8 x 11.8 cm
The Ashmolean Museum, Oxford

Housman published this illustration
to his tale 'Blind Love', which
appeared in the short-lived
periodical *The Pageant* (1897,
p. 125), edited by Geeson White
and Ricketts's partner, the painter
Charles Shannon. The design is one
of Housman's strongest and most
emotive, borrowing from his beloved
Dürer for the battlements and from
the Pre-Raphaelites for the overall
intricacy of his line and finish.

24 **'The Galloping Plough', design for** *The Field of Clover*, 1898

Graphite, pen and Indian ink on
paper mounted on card, initialled
18 x 11.5 cm
Fitzwilliam Museum, Cambridge

This was a truly fanciful volume of
tales. Depicted here is the dullard
Noodle, seen astride his magic
plough as he races away from his
nasty employer. Other tales included
'The Fire Eaters', for which he drew a
crowd of Chinese midgets tumbling
into a burning cottage to gorge
themselves on tongues of fire.

25 **Study for 'The Passionate Puppets' in** *The Field of Clover*, 1898

Pen and ink on tinted paper
11.5 x 6 cm
Private Collection

This rare example of a preliminary
drawing by Housman survives to
indicate his initial freedom in exploring
the composition before the dense pen
line surface defined the composition
for the engraver (see fig. 7).

26 **'The Burning Rose', in**
The Field of Clover, 1898

Proof wood-engraving by
Clemence Housman after a
design by Laurence Housman
11.5 x 7.3 cm
Private Collection

Housman's bravura pen work
often depicted swirling drapery
and dense foliage at the
expense of clarity. Here the
figure appears almost lost in a
maze of line and texture. It
illustrated Housman's own
story 'The Bound Princess' in
this, his third published
collection of such tales.

27 'Of imitating Christ and Despising all the Vanities of the World', 1899

Proof wood-engraving by Clemence Housman after designs by Laurence Housman, published in an edition of Thomas a Kempis's *Of the Imitation of Christ*, 1899
14.4 x 8 cm
Private Collection

Housman's spare architectural drawings for this favourite book are unique to his *oeuvre*. Although he employed elements of Renaissance architecture to frame his figures, a technique also used by his rival Charles Ricketts, Housman inserted his own elongated and tormented characters. Beardsley, the religious convert, also loved this book, and towards the end of his short life he refused to travel without his copy: the story of the gradual progress of a soul to Christian perfection, its detachment from the world and its union with God held especial meaning and comfort for the young invalid artist.

28 **'The Rat Catcher's Daughter'**
in *The Blue Moon*, 1904

Pen and Indian ink, initialled
15.2 x 9.2 cm
Tate. Purchased 1924

This drawing was published in Housman's fourth
and last collection of fairy tales *The Blue Moon*
(1904). Here he borrowed heavily from his favourite
Pre-Raphaelites for figures and the densely darkened
atmosphere of Sixties School illustrators, like his
beloved Arthur Boyd Houghton. His bewitching tale
of a greedy, gold-obsessed rat-catcher who sells his
beautiful daughter to a gold mining gnome was one
of Housman's more bizarre inventions.

29 **'The White Doe'**
in *The Blue Moon*, 1904

Pen and Indian ink, initialled
14 x 8.3 cm
Tate. Purchased 1924

Also published in *The Blue Moon*, this and the
other nine drawings for the volume, again
wood-engraved by his sister Clemence, were
his most subtle in line and shade, preserving
the ethereal nature of such stories as 'The
Way of the Wind', the title story 'The Blue
Moon', filled with elaborate colour imagery,
and 'A Chinese Fairy Tale'.

Charles Ricketts, ARA (1866–1931)

One of the giants of the private press movement and a talented artist and illustrator as well as publisher, stage designer and writer, Ricketts was an enormous influence upon turn-of-the-century Britain. With his lifelong partner, the painter Charles Shannon, he created a salon of influence which included most of the period's finest artistic and literary talents, often publishing their efforts at his Vale Press.

30 EDMUND DULAC

'RI-KE-TSAN-DCHA-NHO-N' (Being a humorous portrait of Charles Ricketts and Charles Shannon as Hindu Gods), 1914

Watercolour
29 cm in diameter
Fitzwilliam Museum, Cambridge

The artistic duo Ricketts and Shannon exerted a tremendous influence over the illustrative arts in England for many years. Their soirées were famously attended by ambitious colleagues like the young impressionable Laurence Housman, who was frightened away, and later Edmund Dulac, the French expatriate who remained devoted to the couple. Here Dulac, in a typically acerbic caricature, depicts the couple with four arms holding a variety of brushes and pens; Shannon clutches a tiny scroll celebrating Ricketts's appointment as ARA (Associate of the Royal Academy).

31 **'Oedipus and
the Sphinx', 1891**

Pen and Indian ink and white,
signed bottom right 'CR 1891'
23.6 x 15.5 cm
Tullie House Museum and Art
Gallery

Ricketts believed this to be his
best drawing, done for a
commission by the highly
respectable academic painter
Sir Frederic Leighton ('I'm
afraid you won't care for my
work, but I am interested in
yours,' Leighton told him). The
drawing depicts the Sphinx, a
classical monster who ravaged
the neighbourhood of Thebes,
devouring all who failed to
answer her riddle. Oedipus
gave the correct answer,
causing the Sphinx to expire,
and was rewarded with the
hand of Jocasta, his widowed
mother. Some believe it to be
among the first true Symbolist
drawings produced in England.

32 'The Labyrinth in which the
Twy-formed Bull was Stalled'
in *The Sphinx*, 1894

Pen and grey wash
on pink prepared paper
19.3 x 16.8 cm
The Ashmolean Museum, Oxford

This exquisite pen drawing was
produced for Ricketts's edition of
Oscar Wilde's *The Sphinx* (1894),
published by Elkin Mathews and John
Lane. Ricketts considered his designs
the best he had ever done, but Wilde
thought differently. This drawing was
owned by Charles Shannon.

33 'Crouching by the Marge'
in *The Sphinx*, 1894

Pen and grey ink
on pink prepared paper
20.2 x 16.4 cm
The Ashmolean Museum, Oxford

The introduction here of a stylised
landscape and spare, almost oriental
starkness made this one of Ricketts'
most unusual illustrations when it
appeared in his edition of Oscar
Wilde's *The Sphinx* (1894).

34 **'Psyche in the House'**
in *De Cupidinus et Psyches*
Amoribus, **1901**

Pen and Indian ink and white,
signed bottom right 'CR'
10.5 x 9.6 cm
Tullie House Museum and Art
Gallery

This original drawing was for the wood-
engraved illustration from the second Latin
edition of the Vale Press's Cupid and Psyche –
De Cupidinus et Psyches Amoribus, published
by Ricketts in 1901. Its strong adherence to
the claustrophobic Pre-Raphaelite formula of
a longhaired medieval maiden in a darkened
room was originally narrower in format:
Ricketts added the left-hand drapery and
expanded the square composition for the
published version. The drawing was originally
reproduced in *The Pageant* in 1896, then
recycled five years later.

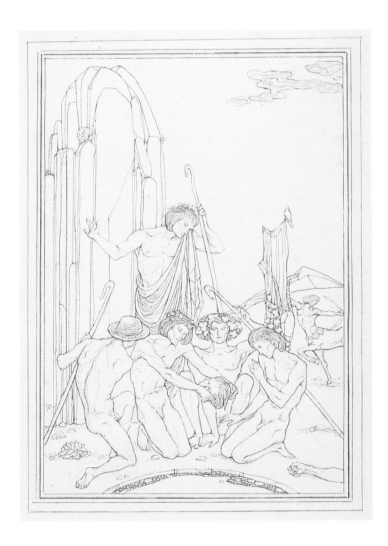

35 'The Head of Orpheus'
in *Beyond the Threshold*, 1929

Pen and Indian ink and white, signed bottom left 'CR'
22.2 x 16.2 cm
Tullie House Museum and Art Gallery

This homage to male beauty was drawn as one of five illustrations for Ricketts's last illustrated book, *Beyond the Threshold* (1929), a series of decadent dialogues in the style of Wilde and Petronius Arbiter. The book's Art Deco-styled, gold-blocked, maroon morocco binding suggested how Ricketts, just two years before his death, was still capable of incorporating the ideas of a new age.

36 'The Birth of Pandora'
in *Beyond the Threshold*, 1929

Pen and Indian ink, signed bottom right 'CR'
23 x 16.8cm
Tullie House Museum and Art Gallery

This late illustration was also published in *Beyond the Threshold*. Towards the end of his life he turned back to his early fine-lined ink style, incorporating favourite themes from the Old Masters he loved. Even here, however, one sees the influence of Art Deco stylisation in the attenuated figures and rocks that give this near religious composition its modern power.

IN THE GOTHIC SHADOW OF BEARDSLEY

Beardsley's death unleashed a stream of devoted disciples determined to emulate and enhance his work. Many chose his more Gothic themes and, using his spare, black and white orientalist aesthetic, they created a series of unique grisly scenes of supernatural horror. The bizarre coalminer-turned-artist Sidney Sime was so inspired by the scratchings he made on the coal surface that he trained in Beardsley's footsteps and eventually created some of the most fantastical drawings of the Beardsley school. Similarly the Irishman Harry Clarke perfected an impish fantasy world as grotesque as it was charming. Both artists represented the best interpreters of a popular strain of Gothic horror and fantasy, drawing with meticulous care, largely in pen and ink, their homages to their mentor Aubrey Beardsley.

Sidney Sime (1867–1941)

One of the more extraordinary artist disciples of Beardsley was the ambitious young Sidney Sime. Despite his humble background, he was a charming character devoted to magazine illustration – he later owned and edited his own illustrated paper, and he had the good fortune to enjoy the support of the wealthy young Irish patron Lord Dunsany, whose fantastical tales he illustrated. A seemingly perfect match of eccentric artist and obsessive writer, their collaborations delighted a small coterie of followers and set the benchmark for the best in Gothic fantasy.

37 **'The Felon Flower', from** **_The Legend of Mandrake_, _c._1897**

Pen and Indian ink, signed
37.8 x 26 cm
Victoria and Albert Museum

Published in _Eureka_ (September 1897), this bizarre composition with its couple and their dog gazing towards the viewer is in strict contrast to the horror described in the poem by the suitably named Knight Ryder.

38 **'The Mermaid',** *c.***1897**

Pen and Indian ink and white heightening on
grey-green card, signed
24.3 x 16.5 cm
Fitzwilliam Museum, Cambridge

Beardsley's last *Volpone* and *Mademoiselle de
Maupin* illustrations were the contemporary
influences in this remarkable drawing, which first
appeared in *Eureka* in autumn 1897, then
reappeared in an article about Sime ('The
Apotheosis of the Grotesque') in *The Idler* in January
1898, a year before Sime bought the magazine.

39 **'The Zagabog' in** *Fancy Free*,
1901

Pen and Indian ink
34 x 22.8 cm
Kendra and Allan Daniel Collection

Sime often adopted botanical themes
to suit his more bizarre creations as
they gave him greater scope for
atmosphere and invention. This
strange invention appeared in Eden
Phillpott's *Fancy Free* (1901), and was
Sime's first published book
illustration.

40 'The sudden discovery of that infamous den', *c*.1901

Pen and Indian ink, wash and white heightening, signed
53.5 x 38 cm
Victoria and Albert Museum

Published as part of the series 'The Fantasy of Life. As seen by S. H. Sime. Drawings to the Unknown Tales' in *The Tatler* (28 August 1901), this grisly scene combines the horror of the boiling pot with touches of typical Sime humour, especially in his rendition here of the devilish helpers.

41 'The Dollar Princess', *c*.1910

Graphite, pen and Indian ink and grey wash, signed
35.6 x 26.5 cm
Fitzwilliam Museum, Cambridge

Sime loved the theatre and produced various designs for plays, such as Maeterlinck's *The Blue Bird*, although he largely drew upon the theatre for general inspiration. Here is one of eight drawings he made for the series 'The Aura of the Drama', published in *The Sketch* on 30 March 1910, the series running between 16 March and 4 May. The text which accompanied this drawing told the story of the Fox and the Goose in the Garden of Opulence, 'instigated by an imitation Eros'.

42 'The Wily Grasser', from *Bogey Beasts*, 1923

Pen and Indian ink and grey wash
22.7 x 17 cm
Fitzwilliam Museum, Cambridge

This disconsolate chicken-like beast was one of fifteen weird creatures Sime invented, twelve of which were first published as 'The Sime Zoology: Beasts That Might Have Been' in *The Sketch* (18 January–22 March 1905). They were later published with music ('for any child with nerve left to raise a voice in song') in the now rare volume, *Bogey Beasts* (1923).

Harry Clarke (1889–1931)

The multi-talented Irishman Harry Clarke was a key figure in bringing the Beardsley religion to Ireland, where he adopted it for book illustrations and the large stained glass designs he coloured and painted for his family firm. A master draughtsman with a fluid line and a trademark wide-eyed figure style, Clarke was a masterful illustrator, who transformed Beardsley's high Gothic line into new depths of depravity and invention, as seen in his Edgar Allan Poe drawings.

43–48 **Six illustrations to Alexander Pope's**
The Rape of the Lock: A Heroic-Comical poem in five Cantos, 1913

Pencil, pen and Indian ink on white card
National Gallery of Ireland, Dublin

This was Clarke's homage to the deceased Beardsley. Commissioned by Laurence Ambrose Waldron, an admirer and patron of young Clarke's work, the series was never published. While comparisons were made with Beardsley's early version of Pope's *Rape of the Lock* (1896), each artist portrayed different aspects of eighteenth-century decoration and costume.

43

'Her guardian sylph prolong'd the balmy rest:'
['Twas he had summon'd to her silent bed
The morning-dream that hover'd o'er her head;]
'A Youth more glittering than a birth-night beau,
(That e'en in slumber caus'd her cheek to glow)
Seem'd to her ear his winning lips to lay,'
[Canto 1st]
27.8 x 17.7 cm

This same passage was chosen by Beardsley for his rendition of the tale, although here Clarke's guardian youth really is an unearthly sylph, with peacock feather wings, and the diaphanous Belinda is seen in bed. Below each drawing Clarke drew the text in pencil, illustrated in Gothic script, filling the margins with whimsical pencil caricatures.

44

'Now awful beauty puts on all its arms;
The fair, each moment, rises in her charms,
Repairs her smiles, awakens every grace,
And calls forth all the wonders of her face;' [Canto 1st]
28 x 17.7 cm

A variant to Beardsley's toilet scene, here Clarke is less
assured, drawing with a more nervous line, his
composition flatter, with static figures behind Belinda's
extravagant crinoline dress.

45

'He takes the gift with reverence, and extends
The little engine on his fingers' ends
This just behind Belinda's neck he spread,
As o'er the fragrant steams she bends her head' [Canto 3rd]
28 x 17.8 cm

Another scene also chosen by Beardsley. Here Clarke gave his
characters a more jaded, dissipated appearance in contrast to
Beardsley's more corpulent, rakish men and fleshy women.
His Baron is nonchalantly snipping off the Lock among the
curling ostrich feathers, as if he can hardly bear the effort of
lifting the scissors ('the little engine on his fingers' ends').

46

'Down to the central earth, his proper scene,
Repair'd to search the gloomy cave of Spleen
[Swift on his sooty pinions flits the gnome,
And in a vapour reach'd the dismal dome.
No cheerful breeze this sullen region knows,
The dreaded east is all the wind that blows.
Here in a grotto, shelter'd close from air,
And screen'd in shades from day's detested glare,
She sighs for ever on her pensive bed,
Plain at her side, and Megrin at her head.]
'Two handmaids wait the throne; alike in place,
But differing far in figure and in face.
Here stood Ill-nature like an ancient maid,
Her wrinkled form in black and white arrayed.'
[With store of pray'rs, for mornings, nights and noons,
Her hand is fill'd; her bosom with lampoons.]
'There Affectation, with a sickly mien,
Shows in her cheeks the roses of eighteen.'
[Canto 4th]
27.8 x 17.8 cm

This dazzling piece of virtuoso penwork suggests
Clarke greatly enjoyed this more fantastical sequence
and it set the pace for a lifelong love of the bizarre in
future inventions. Clarke's biographer best describes
this scene: 'The flitting gnome, swathed in ectoplasmic,
silken strands, with peacock feather wings and wand, is
a master stroke. Spleen also wears billowing strands,
bound at her neck and ankles, as she sits on her snakey
bed. Both Affectation and Ill Nature, the latter with her
checked bag of prayers, and bosom full of lampoons
drawn in the shape of two vipers, are splendid.'

47

'See fierce Belinda on the Baron flies
With more than usual lightning in her eyes'
[Canto 5th]
28 x 18 cm

With this illustration's striking composition
and spare background and foreground,
Clarke again echoed Beardsley, but gave the
bewigged women and gentlemen and their
rococo fripperies (described by Kenneth
Clark as 'ersatz eighteenth century') a less
decorative approach than his mentor's
version of the tale.

48

'But trust the Muse. She saw it upward rise,
Though mark'd by none but quick poetic eyes.'
[So Rome's great founder to the heav'ns withdrew,
To Proculus alone confess'd in view]
'A sudden star, it shot through[h] liquid air,
And drew behind a radiant trail of hair.'
[Canto 5th]
27.9 x 17.9 cm

The soulful Muse, decked in waves of hair with the relics
of the drama before her, watches the apotheosis of the
raped lock, as it is borne up heavenward by a star,
attended by a pair of tiny will-o'-the-wisps.

49 'They swarmed upon me in ever accumulating heaps', from Edgar Allan Poe's *Tales of Mystery and Imagination*

London: George Harrap, 1919
Private Collection

Published as one of several full-page plates, this horrific account of 'The Pit and the Pendulum' was a wonderfully Gothic vision of the ultimate torture.

50 'With magic key, in the evening light, You are unlocking buds that keep the roses', 1920

Pen and Indian ink, signed
20.5 x 15.5 cm
Private Collection

This delightful oval fantasy is reminiscent of Beardsley's late stipple compositions. It illustrated the poem "To the Coming Spring" by Margaret MacKenzie in *The Year's at the Spring* (1920). One can also see Clarke's preoccupation with stained glass design in the drawing's overall oval-shaped composition.

51 Falstaffian figure, 1929

Pencil and watercolour on board,
inscribed 'Arabesque with unsuited
limbs and appointments'
33.5 x 22 cm
Private Collection

This is one of the last drawings
Clarke ever made. Following the
publication of his illustrated edition
of Swinburne poems in late 1928, he
left for a clinic at Davos, Switzerland
to attempt to cure his tuberculosis.
He returned in 1930 and again in
1931, when he died there. During his
confinement, depressed by inactivity
and being divorced from reality,
Clarke eventually recovered enough
to work on stained glass designs for
his family firm, and costume designs
for a ballet, as well as this
watercolour, and another similar
Shakespearean-themed drawing of
Prince Prospero.

FAIRYLAND FANTASY

As a foil to the grotesque, some artists sought the refreshing naivety of childhood, the innocence of folk tale and fairyland which had delighted children for generations. By the turn of the century the belief in fairies had taken a firm hold, not only over children but also their parents. Even the most respectable pillars of society, like Sir Arthur Conan Doyle and the artist Bernard Sleigh, came out in favour of fairyland, and of course Peter Pan haunted the London stage. The sensitivity of a pastel-tinged world filled with flowers and children created by the Scottish artists Jessie King and her Glasgow School of Art colleague Annie French captivated a public tired of dour and dark Victoriana. These two women alone created a series of strikingly feminine watercolours: ethereal, jewel-like and meticulous, they were a distinctive vision of a fairyland filled with legends and folk tales, or just simply celebratory hymns to a gentle innocence which would inspire numerous imitators. As Glasgow School craftswomen they also designed jewellery, furniture, ceramics and the graphic arts, giving a welcome boost to the careers of many of the period's women artists.

Bernard Sleigh (1872–1954)

52 'The Horns of Elfland Faintly Blowing', *c.*1900

Chiaroscuro woodcut, monogrammed
22 x 38 cm
Private Collection

The text for this extraordinary print reads: 'O! Hark O! Hear! How Thin & Clear & Thinner Clearer Farther Going: O! Sweet & Far From Cliff & Scar The Horns of Elfland Faintly Blowing'. Bernard Sleigh was a master woodcut artist and pivotal figure of the turn-of-the-century woodcut revival, and he produced various dramatic prints for literary and artistic magazines and books. Here he skilfully perfected the colour-engraved background of clouds and stars using several blocks to emulate his beloved medieval masters. More to the point, in later life Sleigh discovered fantasy and produced three volumes of engraved fairy subjects inspired by his strong belief in fairies. His unpublished autobiography was in fact entitled *Memoirs of a Human Peter Pan*.

THE GLASGOW SCHOOL ARTISTS

The Glasgow School of Art fostered the decorative arts and created influential talents like Jessie King, her husband E. A. Taylor and Annie French. Students designed furniture, decorative objects, jewellery, ceramics, fabrics and books in preparation for careers in the commercial world. The Glasgow Style was perfected here, notably by 'The Four': the sisters Margaret and Frances Macdonald, and the architects and part-time students Charles Rennie Mackintosh and Herbert MacNair, who were also nicknamed 'The Spooks' from their manner of working and the subject matter of their designs. The Glasgow Style became the inspiration for some of the most advanced turn-of-the-century designs in Britain, Secessionist Europe and, through the work of Frank Lloyd Wright, in America.

53 Attributed to
FRANCES MACDONALD
Angel mirror, c.1900

Beaten lead, wood and mirror
63 x 107 cm
Private Collection

This fine example of Glasgow School craftsmanship emerged from a school whose curriculum, intended to train a new generation of decorative artists, included metalwork design, stained glass, leatherwork, textile printing and ceramics.

Jessie Marion King (1875–1949)

The multi-talented Scot Jessie King represented a new generation of women artists who were accepted for their craftsmanship as well as their unique sense of invention. Obsessed by medievalism and fairy tales, her work embraced both themes and covered a multitude of media, from delicate paintings on vellum, innovative book design, charmingly naive painted pottery, jewellery, batik printing, fashion design and even children's toys.

54 ERNEST ARCHIBALD
TAYLOR
Portrait of Jessie M. King

Black crayon heightened with white over French newsprint
9.2 x 11.8 cm
Rachel Moss

This charming and poignant portrait was drawn by the artist's husband, Ernest Archibald Taylor, whom she met as a fellow student at the Glasgow School of Art and married in 1908. Taylor was a noted critic, stained glass and furniture designer and architect and an important influence upon Jessie King's decorative designs.

55 'The White Lady', *c.*1903

Pen and ink, heightened with silver, on vellum
24.6 x 14.2 cm
Trustees of The Cecil Higgins Art Gallery, Bedford

This early work in the silver stipple technique reminiscent of medieval manuscript illumination suggested where Jessie King's style would take her in future years.

56 **'The Sleeping Beauty',** *c.* 1911–20

Pen and ink and watercolour on
vellum, signed
28.5 x 23.5 cm
Private Collection

Jessie King was inspired by children's
fairy tales, and she often created her
own ethereal world far from their
grim seventeenth-century origins.
The abbreviated form of Perrault's
'The Sleeping Beauty' was well-known
by the nineteenth century, and by
1904 Walter Crane had produced his
own versified version. Jessie King's
version was done between
1911–1920.

57 **'The Sea Voices', 1914**

Pen and ink, watercolour, silver
on vellum
18.4 x 26.1 cm
Victoria and Albert Museum

This charming drawing was
one of fifteen Jessie King
created for a New Year's
supplement to *The Studio*
(January 1914) to accompany
verses from John Davidson's
'Seven Happy Days' and other
poets. Such delicate work
could now be easily
reproduced photomechanically
in magazines without losing
definition.

58 **'The Enchanted Faun' or
'The Magic Fawn'**

Fan-shaped pen and ink and
watercolour on vellum, signed
27 x 53.5 cm
Private Collection

This was a favourite subject and
one Jessie King also developed
for an early (c.1904) mosaic
panel of coloured and mirror
glass, using a technique her
husband was particularly skilled
at perfecting. This drawing is
from her late period (1921–49).

59 *The High History of the Holy Graal*

Translated from the Old French by Septimus Evans
London: J. M. Dent and Company, 1903
Private Collection

This was Jessie King's first major book illustration commission, and although her performance was uneven, the best of her 23 full-page illustrations printed in black and red filled the spaces admirably. The volume was intended for the expensive gift book market and issued by Dent in two editions: a standard trade edition and an elaborate deluxe vellum-bound edition for collectors.

61 **Doll's House, 1913**

Painted wood
47 x 71.2 x 29.2 cm
Victoria and Albert Museum

Designed by Jessie King in the Glasgow Style, this was part of a child's nursery she created to accompany a major exhibition in Paris, *Exposition de l'Art pour l'Enfance* at the Musée Galliera. She in fact designed the entire nursery, complete with furnishings, furniture, a frieze and stained glass window (fig. 12). In later life she also lectured about toy-making, recalling how adept she was at an early age at cabinet-making and carpentry.

60 *The Defence of Guenevere and Other Poems*

By William Morris
London: John Lane, The Bodley Head, 1904
Private Collection

This was the book that made Jessie King's reputation as a book illustrator. Commissioned by Beardsley's publisher John Lane, she created 95 line drawings as well as designing the exquisite binding.

Annie French (1872–1965)

A colleague of Jessie King's at the Glasgow School of Art, Annie French was an inventive and innovative watercolourist and later a greetings card designer. She perfected a gentle, almost ethereal watercolour stipple style which suggests the early stipple engravings so beloved by Beardsley for his eighteenth-century pastiches.

62 **'The Daisy Chain'**, *c.*1916

Pen and ink on vellum, signed
17.7 x 37.1 cm
Victoria and Albert Museum

This was a typical subject for the artist who, with Jessie King, developed a vein of charming whimsicality which was missing in the works of their fellow Glasgow School artists. Floral and fairy tale subjects predominated, which gave Annie French enough scope to create intricate, jewel-like works of a unique, almost medieval manuscript quality.

63 'A Fairy Tale'

Pen and ink and watercolour, signed
21.2 x 25.7 cm
Private Collection

The air of mystery inherent in this delightful watercolour's title is typical of Annie French's light-hearted approach to her work. She revelled in childish themes and transformed them with her unique series of tight, intricate brushwork dots and pale, subdued palette.

64 'The Queen and the Gypsies'

Pen and ink and watercolour, signed
23 x 30.8 cm
Private Collection

The popular strain of medievalism so beloved by her colleague Jessie King was also embraced by Annie French, although the latter's approach was more ethereal and less Germanic.

THE AGE OF ENCHANTMENT

With the rise in the lavish colour-plate gift book market, a new generation of artist-illustrators transformed the black and white visions of Beardsley into a healthier, multicoloured world of fairy tale and fantasy which appealed to a younger, more optimistic generation of book buyers. Artists became household names, their annual illustrated books eagerly awaited and usually issued in both an expensive lavishly-bound collectors' edition, limited and signed by the artist, and a less expensive trade edition, which often sold thousands of copies. The illustrated gift book of the 1900–30 period was indeed big business. Moreover the artists often sold their original artwork at the specially themed publicity exhibitions in London's prestigious Bond Street, which gave them an extra income and helped to fan the flames of their fame. Many of the works shown here were bought from these exhibitions.

Arthur Rackham, RI (1867–1939)

Although Arthur Rackham is generally recognised to be the master of the twentieth-century illustrated colour-plate book, the creator of signature trees and grotesque creatures, he often turned to the sea for inspiration. Although he never lived near the sea, he found in later years it helped to inspire his Art Nouveau visions of his most favourite adult subjects, including the plays of Shakespeare and the legends of Wagner. For these he often incorporated nubile young women in scenes of a veiled eroticism which upset his loyal parental following. He called upon the sinewy Art Nouveau aesthetic used by the sculptors and ceramic artists popular at the time, as is represented here, and created some of the most memorable images of the colour illustrated gift book.

65 'The Widow Whitgift and her Sons', 1906

Pen and ink, watercolour, signed
30.8 x 24.5 cm
Victoria and Albert Museum

Here Rackham uses his own love of the sea and parodies the period's Newlyn School painters of fishermen and Cornish coastal life made famous by Stanhope Forbes and others. Interestingly, it was intended to illustrate a story by Rudyard Kipling, 'The Dymchurch Flit' published in Kipling's *Puck of Pook's Hill* in an exclusive American edition. The lure of fairies was still a popular conceit in artistic circles of this period and Rackham rose to the occasion with this splendid beachside vision.

66 'Lizzie, Lizzie, have you tasted, For my sake the fruit forbidden?' in *Goblin Market*, 1933

Pen and ink and watercolour, signed
26.6 x 19.5 cm
Private Collection

Published in Christina Rossetti's *Goblin Market* (1933) alongside three other colour illustrations, Rackham's rendition of the classic tale of lost innocence, sisterly love and seduction (first illustrated by the author's brother Dante Gabriel, then by Laurence Housman) remained a challenge to Rackham's inventive powers. Unlike Housman's more successful brooding creatures, his are rather twee woodland elves and furry cats and rats who appear to be more jovial than threatening. Here too, in the figure of Lizzie, we have Rackham's late preoccupation with nubile young women.

67 **'The Rhine-Maidens teasing Alberich' from Rackham's edition of Richard Wagner's** *The Rhinegold and The Valkyrie*

London: William Heinemann, 1910
Private Collection

One of 30 colour plates Rackham created for this adult-themed volume, here he embraced the Art Nouveau design aesthetic which was so popular at the time, especially among the French decorative arts.

68 RAOUL FRANCOIS LARCHE
'The Sirens', *c.*1900

Bronze
37 x 26 cm
Private Collection

The fluid forms of the French Art Nouveau
sculptor Raoul Larche (1860–1912) suggest
how Rackham borrowed from the period's
aesthetic for his own designs of Wagnerian
underwater frolics. Here the screaming
sirens are a terrifying yet powerful reminder
of the lure of classical legend. Larche was a
prominent Art Nouveau sculptor who
specialised in such watery, emotive subjects
as 'The Pool'. He is most noted, however, for
his Art Nouveau masterpiece, the influential
bronze of the famed veil dancer Loie Fuller
(*c.*1900) now in the Musée des Arts
Decoratifs, Paris, with its fluid lines and
ethereal pose.

69 EMILE GREGOIRE
'Undine'

Unglazed ceramic
70 x 32 cm
Private Collection

Emile Gregoire (b. 1871, fl. 1890s) was a noted French sculptor
famed for allegorical works like this, and another he called
'Captivity'. He was hugely successful and won the Prix de Rome
in 1899. Here he poses the legendary figure Undine, the female
water sprite found in forest pools and waterfalls. Famed for her
seductive and beautiful voice, legend has it she could sometimes
be heard over the sound of falling water, plaintively calling in
search of her mate for, according to that same legend, she must
marry a human to receive a soul. Undine was a favourite legend
of Queen Victoria, who once presented the water sprite's portrait
to her beloved Prince Albert. This sculpture suggests how popular
taste in decorative objects for the home embraced the watery
world of legends, which in turn inspired artists like Rackham to
create their own two-dimensional underworld. His illustrated
edition of *Undine* was published in 1909.

Charles Robinson, RI
(1870–1937)

One of the period's finest children's illustrators, Charles Robinson was long associated with visions of cherubic children and their adoring mothers, set amongst lavish gardens and floral displays. A master at pen and ink and atmospheric watercolour, he was prolific too (between 1905 and 1909 he illustrated some 39 books). His books sold in great numbers and offered strong competition to Rackham, who was his exact contemporary. Today his work is largely overshadowed by that of his older brother, William Heath Robinson.

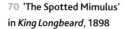

70 'The Spotted Mimulus'
in *King Longbeard*, 1898

Pen and ink
36.8 x 25.5 cm
Private Collection

Published in B. MacGregor's *King Longbeard* (1898), this typified the young Robinson's early attempts to illustrate for the booming children's market. Prolific even at this early stage in his career, this same year he published *Lilliput Lyrics*, *Richard Wagner and The Ring*, an edition of Hans Andersen's *Fairy Tales*, illustrated with his brother, and four other books.

71 **'The house was filled with slaves bearing basons of massy gold'**, from *Aladdin, or The Wonderful Lamp*

Pen, ink, watercolour and bodycolour, signed
37.1 x 26.9 cm
Victoria and Albert Museum

This splendidly exotic subject served as the frontispiece to *The Big Book of Fairy Tales*, published by Blackie and Sons in 1911. The designs were bordered in a rich 'Islamic' arched patterning reminiscent of Persian miniatures, with the text worked into the lower portion of the border.

"The house was filled with slaves bearing basons of massy gold". *Aladdin.*

72 '**Tended the garden from morn to even**' from *The Sensitive Plant*, 1912

Colour plate from Percy Bysshe Shelley's *The Sensitive Plant*
London: William Heinemann, 1912
Private Collection

This was one of Robinson's most successful floral fantasies, published as a full-page plate 'tipped in' to one of his most endearing books.

73 **Binding design to Anatole France's**
Bee: The Princess of the Dwarfs **retold in**
English by Peter Wright

London: J. M. Dent and Sons Ltd., 1912
Private Collection

Charles Robinson's signature style of
cherubic infants and children endeared
him to an older generation of parents
intent upon buying his numerous titles.

74 **'The rich making merry in their**
beautiful houses while the beggars
were sitting at the gates' from
The Happy Prince and other Tales, 1913

Pen, ink, watercolour and bodycolour
36.9 x 27 cm
Victoria and Albert Museum

This is one of Robinson's illustrations to Oscar Wilde's
The Happy Prince and other Tales, published by
Duckworth. Here the influence of Japanese prints,
combined with subtle handling of colour and scale,
suggests Robinson was experimenting with a stage set-
like composition, juxtaposing the Pre-Raphaelite-inspired
red-haired maiden in the foreground with the appealing
glow of the candlelit interior. Despite its darkness, this is
one of Robinson's most powerful works.

75 'Peggy and Tim arrive at the bottom' from *The Goldfish Bowl*, 1922

Watercolour, signed
32 x 26.6 cm
Private Collection

This illustration to P. Austin's *The Goldfish Bowl* (1922) is indicative of Robinson's love of innocence which translated into an endearing approach to the children's book market, where he secured, by pure hard work and numerous publications, a premier position.

76 'The Siesta'

Pen and Indian ink, inscribed and signed
31.2 x 53.1 cm
Private Collection

Robinson could be masterful at pen draughtsmanship, and he created some wonderfully large ink drawings, inventive, free and clearly inspired by a vivid imagination. Critics today put this down to his being largely self-taught.

THE ENCHANTMENT OF NATURE

With Edwardian prosperity came a longing for escape from the confines of factory-choked cities. Suburban sprawl brought commuters into the idyllic English countryside, while the railways gave day-trippers the opportunity to explore the landscape and wildlife, and publishers quickly responded to their demands for credible escapist literature. Artists made their careers painting popular rural subjects or drawing the aspects of Mother Nature which now held such an especial fascination for the burgeoning middle classes. The masters of this new genre were the extraordinary twin brothers, the Detmolds. Their superb prints, book illustrations and paintings remain unrivalled depictions of an almost surreal approach to nature.

Charles Maurice Detmold (1883–1908) and Edward Julius Detmold (1883–1956)

The Detmold twins were child prodigies. Their artful yet remarkably accurate depictions of plant, animal and insect life were begun in their early teens, while experimenting with the etching process. They quickly mastered the technique and turned instead to illustration, creating fanciful watercolours for colour-plate books like their exotic subjects for Rudyard Kipling's *Jungle Book*. Their collaborations ended tragically when Charles Maurice (known professionally as Maurice) committed suicide in 1908, leaving his bereft brother to continue their work and develop further the distinctive exoticism which always permeated their work.

77 EDWARD DETMOLD
'Charles Maurice Detmold',
1899

Pencil, signed and dated
31.4 x 24.8 cm
© reserved; collection
National Portrait Gallery,
London

78 MAURICE DETMOLD
'Edward Julius Detmold',
1899

Pencil, monogrammed and
dated
25.8 x 17.5 cm
© National Portrait Gallery,
London

These two remarkably sensitive portraits, drawn when the twin artists were just sixteen, were commissioned by the art critic and journalist M. H. Spielmann for his laudatory article, 'Two Boys – Maurice and Edward Detmold', in the *Magazine of Art* (1900, pp.112–18). In it he waxed lyrical about these young protégés and described their remarkable early achievements, then concluded, 'It rests with themselves to rise – and rise they assuredly will.'

E. J. Detmold   M. Detmold

79 MAURICE AND EDWARD DETMOLD
'The Hornbill'

Colour etching,
signed 'E. J. Detmold and M. Detmold'
6.9 x 10.8 cm
Private Collection

This delicate, orientalist-inspired print, signed to
indicate both brothers had worked the plate, was
issued coloured and uncoloured when it appeared
in their first portfolio, *Eight Proof Etchings* (1898),
which they sold from their Hampstead home. It
quickly sold out and launched their careers as
printmakers. They were just fifteen years old.

80 MAURICE AND EDWARD DETMOLD

'Shere Khan in the Jungle' from *Illustrations to Rudyard Kipling's Jungle Book*

Chromolithograph from a set of sixteen
33 x 21.5 cm
Private Collection

This striking composition illustrated the lines:
'"Fla! Fla!" said Mowgli, on his back. "Now thou knowest!" and the torrent of black horns, foaming muzzles and staring eyes whirled down the ravine like boulders in flood-time; the weaker buffaloes being shouldered out to the sides of the ravine, where they tore through the creepers.'

This portfolio is generally considered to be the Detmold brothers' finest collaborative achievement, hailed by their biographer David Larkin as 'a wonderful production, in green linen with silk ties, the upper cover gilt stamped with a winged beast – the mythic element used by the Detmolds.' He concluded that the watercolour illustrations 'must be among the finest book illustrations ever produced'. Here Edward used bolder outline, borrowing from a love of Japanese prints while Charles Maurice achieved greater depth through shading. Issued by Macmillan as a portfolio of plates without text in 1903, the sixteen plates were masterpieces in this size, but disappointingly poorly printed when later reduced in the full text edition issued in 1908. By then Kipling's original illustrated edition of *The Jungle Book*, published in 1894, had sold 82,000 copies. Such was the popularity of the author that his publisher Macmillan eventually issued 21 separate Kipling titles.

81 MAURICE DETMOLD

'Monkey Fight', 1901, for *Illustrations to Rudyard Kipling's The Jungle Book*, 1903

Watercolour, signed with monogram and dated
58 x 42.5 cm
Private Collection

This original watercolour for the chromolithographic plate illustrates the lines: 'There was a howl of fright and rage, then as Bagheera tripped on the rolling, kicking bodies beneath him, a monkey shouted, "There is only one here! Kill him! Kill!"'

82 EDWARD DETMOLD

'The White Horseman' from *The Arabian Nights*, 1922

Watercolour, pen and ink heightened with gold and bodycolour, signed with monogram
80.3 x 57.8 cm
Private Collection

After the death of his brother, Edward gradually returned to illustration. The twelve large watercolour plates he produced for this volume are among his most fantastical. Delicately coloured and carefully delineated to emulate the exoticism of the East, they were expertly printed using new technologies to reproduce his most atmospheric and exquisite washes. Even today many believe the splendours of the East have rarely been portrayed with such colours and attention to detail. This large and impressive portrait from the tale, 'The History of Codadad and his Brothers and History of the Princess Deryaba' illustrated the lines 'Drawing his scimitar aimed at him a blow which, had it found him, must there and then have ended the fight.' Edward returned to the same powerful subject later and experimented with a series of large, bold, heavily inked etchings of the same horseman.

83 EDWARD DETMOLD
'Tiger, Butterflies, and Fan Palms'

Colour etching
31.6 x 42.4 cm
Private Collection

This is the most impressive print of Edward Detmold's
oeuvre, a technical *tour de force* in which all its colours
were printed from just one plate. It was probably first
inked with green, then wiped clean, leaving traces in
the etched lines, using a technique the French call *à la
poupée*. Local colours were then applied to the plate
in a film of ink which was sufficiently thick so it would
not run. The white of the tiger's fur was produced by
wiping away at the plate, the resulting print becoming
a type of monoprint which was so time-consuming to
produce that Edward limited the edition number
to just twelve impressions.

84 EDWARD DETMOLD
'Parrot'

Colour etching
47.5 x 36.5 cm
Private Collection

This is one of Edward's most
successful and popular bird portraits.
It was produced in an unusually
small edition of twelve, after initially
being editioned at seven, then
selling out. This print is number two.

85 EDWARD DETMOLD
'The Bluebird Fan'

Watercolour on paper
35.5 x 50.8 cm
Private Collection

This highly unusual fan design borrowed heavily from the Japanese influences so beloved by the Detmold twins. It was exhibited at the prestigious Leicester Galleries in London, where their colleagues Rackham, Dulac and Clarke had also exhibited and sold their original illustrations, and was purchased by the present owner at that gallery.

86 EDWARD DETMOLD
'Egrets on the Nile'

Oil on panel
32 x 39 cm
Private Collection

Edward experimented with bird and animal subjects in oil paint on panel during his later years, but his mastery of the medium seemed to defeat his natural tendency for delicacy and finesse.

87 EDWARD DETMOLD
'The Goldfish', 1926

Colour etching, number 2 of 15
11.4 x 12.7 cm
Private Collection

In later life Edward used the goldfish or Japanese koi carp as a colourful subject in the hope he might attract sales to boost his beleaguered career. The seemingly mundane subject was characteristically infused with Detmold magic as the sculptural sea and bubbles surround the etched pair of oriental kois.

88 EDWARD DETMOLD
'Tiger, Tiger'

Gesso (?) over printed (?) background on panel
30.5 x 48.2 cm
Private Collection

This highly unusual 'raised painting' was executed in the 1920s using a technique which even today remains a mystery. The theme, borrowed from William Blake's famous verse 'Tiger, tiger, burning bright', was popular enough for the composition to be reissued later as a fine art print. Edward's fascination with this almost psychedelic palette dominated his later colour work.

89 EDWARD DETMOLD

'Alice in Wonderland with Peter the Lizard'

Pencil and watercolour
36.2 x 29.2 cm
Private Collection

This is one of Edward's more surreal illustrations. In it he incorporated the soft brushwork – almost in emulation of modern airbrushing – with his incomparable knowledge of animals and insects to create a startlingly original pastiche of the classic Alice story.

90–93 EDWARD DETMOLD
Four Fantastical Creatures,
c.1926

Watercolours, signed with initials
20.5 cm diameter each
Private Collection

90 **'An Imaginary Rabbit'** [top left]

91 **'The Bandiscoot Family'** [top right]

92 **'Imaginary Submarine Creature'**
    [bottom left]

93 **'The Cheryl'** [bottom right]

These four watercolours, created around 1926, are undoubtedly the strangest of Edward's entire *oeuvre*. Nothing is known of their inspiration or the source for their bizarre titles. They do indicate his love of the fantastical, marrying his knowledge of natural history with his vivid imagination which allowed him to create these startlingly original creatures.

INTERNATIONAL ENCHANTMENT

With the boom in British publishers' elaborate gift books came the need for new talent to help fuel the growing market. A rich vein of artistic innovation was found abroad: trained in Paris, Germany or even Hungary, a new breed of expatriate artist-illustrators emerged in London, then the publishing capital of Europe, all of them determined to capitalise on these new opportunities and to make their careers. With them came a refreshing new and colourful approach to illustration inspired by Scandinavian and Russian folk tales, the breathtaking productions of the Ballets Russes — whose exotic themes had never before been seen in Britain — and of course the theatre. Émigré artists like the Hungarian Willy Pogany, the Frenchman Edmund Dulac, the Dane Kay Nielsen and the German Alastair created some of the period's finest illustrations, and their work in turn inspired a new generation of British artists and craftsmen.

Willy Pogany (1882–1955)

One of the finest disciples of Rackham, and a new master of the colour-plate book with his own distinctive, highly romantic, often Gothic subjects was the Hungarian artist William Andrew ('Willy') Pogany. A talented mimic of the period's great illustrators, he quickly secured a place in British publishing history, despite the fact that he had only intended to work in London briefly, en route to greener pastures in America. Taken up by the enterprising publisher George Harrap, his elaborate and remarkably subtle colour volumes would quickly rival even his colleague Edmund Dulac's exotic creations.

94 'Part 1 – The Enchantment'

Colour chapter heading from Pogany's illustrated edition of *The Tale of Lohengrin: Knight of the Swan*, after the Drama of Richard Wagner
London: George Harrap, 1913
Private Collection

Pogany was a master of colour illustration in an age when colour printing had never been so accurate. Here he created wonderful atmospheric fantasies to enhance Wagner's highly charged world, which were printed on a cream-tinted paper to emulate age.

95 'The Swan Knight', tailpiece illustration to *Lohengrin*, 1913

Pen and ink
8 x 8 cm
Private Collection

This is one of the many delicate ink drawings Pogany produced for his Wagnerian fantasy. The elongated nude was printed in black, within a box surrounded by a gold border of intricate medieval crests and a stretching swan.

96 'Rumpelstiltskin'

Watercolour, signed
49.8 x 34.5 cm
Private Collection

This popular Grimm fairy tale was just one of several folk tale subjects painted by Pogany in the Edwardian period for the British market. These included an illustrated Goethe's *Faust* (1908), Fitzgerald's *The Rubaiyat of Omar Khayyam* (1909), Nathaniel Hawthorne's *Tanglewood Tales* (1909), *Norse Wonder Tales* (1910) and, appropriately for a native-born Hungarian, *The Hungarian Fairy Book* (1913), compiled by Nandor Pogany.

Edmund Dulac (1882–1953)

Edmund Dulac was undoubtedly the greatest rival to Arthur Rackham for the gift book market. An inveterate Anglophile, Dulac had arrived in London determined to make his mark in publishing, and over his long 50-plus year career he not only mastered the illustrated book, but also design for stage, costume, tapestry, carpet and furniture, as well as for postage stamp and coinage. A master colourist, he took his inspiration from the Orient and Near East and created some of the most colourful illustrations yet published.

97 Edmund Dulac, 1 July 1914

Collotype by Alvin Langdon Coburn
19.5 x 15.9 cm
© reserved; collection National Portrait Gallery, London

This stylish portrait study of Edmund Dulac, taken at the height of his international reputation, suggests his deep passion for the exotic, posed as he is against a painted backdrop of pumas set in a tropical jungle. The French-born Dulac always cut a dapper figure, here with hair carefully coiffed and dressed in a full coat and open-necked shirt and colourful ascot. Dulac was in fact a devoted student of fashion. As a young art student in Paris he adopted what he thought was the English mode of dress: tight trousers, spats, white gloves and a cane. He always wore a wide-brimmed hat, which he tilted at an angle to impress the ladies, practising a raised right eyebrow in the mirror to suggest the air of careless amusement which he adopted, to the delight of his friends, throughout his life.

98–101 Four designs for *Stories from the Arabian Nights*, re-told by Laurence Housman, 1907

98 'Great was the astonishment of the Vizier'

Watercolour, signed
25.9 x 35.7 cm
© copyright the Trustees of the British Museum

99 'He saw black eunuchs lying asleep'

Watercolour, signed
29.1 x 18.1 cm
© copyright the Trustees of the British
Museum

Dulac's 50 colour plates, cover and title design for this version of the *Arabian Nights* were published in 1907 by his new employer, the enterprising gift book publisher Hodder and Stoughton, in both trade and collectors' editions. They quickly made the 25-year-old Dulac's reputation and launched his career as a quality illustrator of elaborate collectors' gift books. With the book's success he was heralded as a sure rival to Arthur Rackham. Its editor Laurence Housman was a master at simplifying fairy tales into symbolist hymns, many emphasising colour and sensation, which greatly appealed to a generation of visually jaded Edwardians. The stories in *The Arabian Nights* continued to be popular long after the Victorians had discovered them, even amongst post-World War One survivors.

These exotic tales were also a particular favourite amongst parents concerned for their children's education, as the foreword to one 1917 edition pointed out: 'No children's library is nowadays complete without its volume of *Arabian Nights,* for in no other collection of tales are the doings of Jinns, Fairies, and Magicians told with such verisimilitude; to this is added the glamour of Oriental scenes and places, and descriptions of customs, habits, and manners of living so dissimilar to those which obtain amongst Western nations. To this day the Arab is a firm believer in the influence of good and evil spirits of both sexes upon the human race, whose powers may be involved by talismans, magic, and necromancy.'

100 'The Cup of Wine she gives him each night'

Watercolour with bodycolour, signed
38.2 x 19.1 cm
© copyright the Trustees of the British Museum

101 'The Doctors or It was in vain that all the best physicians in the country were summoned into consultation'

Watercolour, signed
26 x 30 cm
Private Collection

102 'Madame s'est piqué le doigt', 1907

Watercolour, signed
30 x 42 cm
Private Collection

Dulac's French background inspired many of his
finest bewigged period pastiches. A master of
caricature, he could infuse into his figures, with
just the flick of a brush, the required humour or, in
this case, set the scene for true drawing room
comedy of the type Dulac relished: surely the
prostrate and hugely pampered mistress, who has
apparently just pricked her finger and is examined
by the obsequious physician, belongs to the
legions of the high camp, while the black houseboy
in turban and upturned slippers hints at the exotic
direction Dulac would take his career.

Dulac's *Tempest* illustrations marked
a new development away from mere
coloured narrative towards mood
and tone pictures which won him
critical praise, especially for his
renditions of the sea. The dreamy
atmosphere in 'Such Stuff' (cat.104)
was praised by Dulac's biographer as
'showing the creation of the
Universe from primeval chaos, an
example of pure spontaneously felt
painting which could not possibly
have been done using tracings'.

Dulac created 40 beautifully
observed colour illustrations for this
edition of Shakespeare's *The
Tempest*, published in a new series of
Shakespearean plays by Hodder and
Stoughton in 1908. This was in fact
a companion volume to W. Heath
Robinson's illustrated edition of *The
Twelfth Night*. The book was issued
in a deluxe vellum-bound collectors'
edition of 500 copies, signed by
Dulac, and also a less expensive
trade edition, followed by six
illustrations reprinted from the
book for a Dulac '"The Tempest"
Calendar'.

103 **'The Wreck'**

Watercolour, gouache
and pencil, signed
42.5 x 28 cm
Jeremy and Eski Thomas

104 'We are Such Stuff as
Dreams are Made on'

Watercolour, gouache
and pencil, signed
46.3 x 27.9 cm
Jeremy and Eski Thomas

105 **'The Entomologist's Dream', 1909**

Watercolour, signed
27.2 x 29.8 cm
Victoria and Albert Museum

This delightful 'Blue Period' fantasy was published as one of three illustrations to the French tale 'Le Papillon rouge' in *L'Illustration*, a magazine not unlike the English *Illustrated London News* and owned by Henri Piazza, who became an important Dulac patron. The work was exhibited at the Barcelona International Exhibition in 1911, where it received a gold medal. Here Dulac began to experiment with complimentary colours, enhancing his rich trademark blue background by lightly scribbling with a coarse ochre crayon over the painted surface, a technique he developed further in poster designs, like his *Macbeth* poster (cat. 109).

106 'She found herself face to face with a stately and beautiful lady' from 'Beauty and the Beast' in *The Sleeping Beauty and other Tales*, 1910

Pen, ink and watercolour, signed
32.5 x 26.8 cm
Victoria and Albert Museum

This is one of 30 colour plates for a compilation of tales selected by Arthur Quiller-Couch from the Brothers Grimm and Perrault. The eagerly awaited annual gift book was published in 1910, again by Hodder and Stoughton and to instant and enormous success. It is one of Dulac's best 'Blue Period' illustrations, painted in a decorative style that ranged from orientalism to rococo revival. He relished the chance to pick out the intricate textures of lace and fabric, combined with an obvious nod to historical eighteenth-century accuracy.

107 'She made her escape as lightly as a deer'
from 'Cinderella' in *The Sleeping Beauty and
other Tales*, 1910

Watercolour, signed
31 x 24.5 cm
Kendra and Allan Daniel Collection

For this challenging new commission by Hodder
and Stoughton for 30 colour plates to *The
Sleeping Beauty and other Tales*, Dulac was
determined to find appropriate female models.
He decided upon his new wife Elsa for the round-
faced beauty with a pointed chin in 'Beauty and
the Beast', and used her again as Bluebeard's wife
and as Sleeping Beauty, while Cinderella was
posed by his art-school friend Emile Rixens's new
wife, Lea. In this work Dulac used his familiar
blues but also new combinations of orange and
yellow which suggested how he now began to
experiment with a wider range of colour palette.

108 'Circe' [The Enchantress], 1911

Watercolour, gouache, pen and ink, signed
35.8 x 28.5 cm
Jeremy and Eski Thomas

Dulac's new French patron Henri Piazza
commissioned this striking work. As
proprietor of *L'Illustration*, a French
literary paper which printed fiction, poetry
and news and used the latest colour
printing technologies, Piazza appealed to
Dulac. Here he illustrated classically
inspired poems by Alexandre Dumas like
'Circe', which was inspired by the
enchantress who bewitched Odysseus
and transformed his crew into pigs. This
watercolour was exhibited at Dulac's
annual exhibition at the Leicester Galleries
in 1911 and remains in its original
exhibition frame and gold mount.

Shakespeare's **Macbeth**
his Majesty's Theatre

One of a number of theatrical poster
designs Dulac created over the years,
this was his largest watercolour. It was
produced to advertise Granville Barker's
production of *Macbeth* at Her Majesty's
Theatre, London in 1911. Interestingly
his great friend Charles Ricketts
designed a poster for another Granville
Barker production, Thomas Hardy's *The
Dynasts*. Here Dulac excelled in the
dramatic: his worn Macbeth stands
defiantly over Shakespeare's 'blasted
heath', the strapwork and rivet
decorations eventually published as a
border adding period flavour and
prefiguring the sombre colours of his
version of Edgar Allan Poe's stories,
The Bells (1912).

**110 'It is gold' in *Stories from Hans
Andersen*, 1911**

Watercolour, signed
34.6 x 27.5 cm
Victoria and Albert Museum

This was published in *Stories from Hans
Andersen* (1911), the book that
contained some of Dulac's most
memorable images, like 'The Princess
and the Pea' posed in an enormous bed
above 20 differently patterned
mattresses, or 'The Little Mermaid'
which borrowed heavily from
Rackham's vision of the Rhinemaidens
of the previous year, and his most
famous rendition of 'The Snow Queen'.
So popular was this book that it was
also issued in five smaller booklets,
using a favourite colour image
republished for each of their covers.

111 **'Fairy-land' from the poem 'Fairy-land' in *The Bells and other Poems* by Edgar Allan Poe, 1912**

Watercolour and bodycolour
38.8 x 28.2 cm
Victoria and Albert Museum

With the 28 colour plates and ten pen and ink drawings published in his version of Poe's famous tales, Dulac entered the canon of great Poe interpreters, alongside his rivals Harry Clarke and Arthur Rackham. His interpretation, however, was more colourful, though sombre enough to suggest the horrors of Poe's vision. Critics have noted this uncharacteristic sombre tone reached an emotional pitch seldom seen in Dulac's work, and heralded a new colour direction.

112 'The Raven', from *The Bells and other Poems* by Edgar Allan Poe, 1912

Watercolour and bodycolour, signed
39 x 29 cm
© Copyright the Trustees of The British Museum

Poe's haunting tales could not be successfully interpreted without including his famous raven. Dulac's version, published again as an annual gift book for 1912 by Hodder and Stoughton, was issued in a deluxe collectors' edition of 750 copies.

This delightful compilation of
favourite children's storybook
characters was dated '11' and
was probably intended for
publication but remains
untraced. Masterfully, here
Dulac plays with Western
concepts of pictorial space,
pulling the eye from the
courting couple in the
foreground into the foliage
inhabited by fairies, all the
while allowing for a meticulous
study of each endearing
nursery character.

114 '**The Princess Badoura**', **1913**

Watercolour and bodycolour, signed
28.7 x 23.7 cm
© Copyright the Trustees of The British Museum

Published as the frontispiece to *Princess Badoura: A Tale from the Arabian Nights*, retold by Laurence Housman and published by Hodder and Stoughton (1913), this was a second collaboration with Housman, who had selected tales for Dulac's *Stories from the Arabian Nights* in 1907. This masterful creation, not unlike a scene from a Chinese opera, hinted at Dulac's new preoccupation with the decidedly un-Western use of space by surrounding a figure rather than allowing it to be dictated by the laws of perspective. The story, which merited ten colour plates of exquisite oriental inspiration, was the chilling tale of Scheherazade, who, having amused her husband the Sultan every night for almost three years by relating 1001 tales of fantasy, finally obtained a renunciation of his vow to kill each of his brides the morning after her wedding-night.

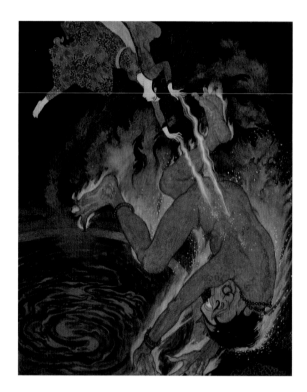

115–118 Four illustrations from *Sinbad the Sailor and other stories of the Arabian Nights*, 1914

115 'The Princess burns the Elfrite to death'

Watercolour, pen and ink and bodycolour
31.5 x 25.2 cm
© Copyright the Trustees of The British Museum

The 23 colour plates Dulac produced for this 1914 gift book, published by Hodder and Stoughton, were among his most colourful and Persian in style. He had just returned from an ecstatic visit to Mediterranean and northern African ports on board his patron's yacht, where he discovered the colourful, exotic world he had previously only imagined. As a result his colours became more vibrant: the blues and greys of earlier Arab street scenes now gave way to tangerines and carmine set against black, or heightened with Chinese white, while his interiors took on a sun-filled vibrancy which he coupled with the intricacies he borrowed from Persian miniatures and architecture. Pictorial space became a preoccupation and he began to tilt his surfaces forward, and he reinforced his picture planes by making both the background and foreground colours equally strong, foreshortening frontal views of surfaces with distant objects painted the same size as nearer ones, and stylised objects themselves with strong patterns.

116 'Sinbad the Sailor entertains Sinbad the Landsman' – used as the book's frontispiece

Watercolour, signed
32.7 x 25.8 cm
Kendra and Allan Daniel Collection

117 'The room of fruits prepared for Abu-l-Hasan', 1914

Watercolour, signed
36 x 28.5 cm
Private Collection

118 'Abu-l-Hasan awakes'

Watercolour
35 x 28 cm
Private Collection

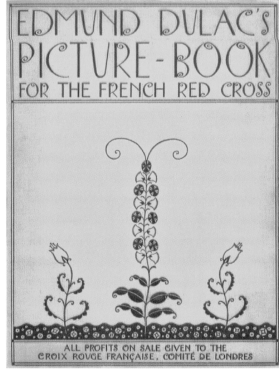

119 **'The Ice Maiden', or 'Everything about her was white', 1915**

Watercolour and bodycolour, signed
30.5 x 25.4 cm
Royal Pavilion, Libraries and Museums, Brighton and Hove

As part of the war effort, Dulac agreed to provide select illustrations, often from previously published works, for various topical and charitable publications. This fine fantasy was freshly painted and remains a remarkable *tour de force* as one of six illustrations he created to illustrate *The Dreamer of Dreams* by Queen Marie of Romania. His publisher Hodder and Stoughton produced this nationalistic volume in 1915, the year that Romania had just joined the Allies, and, no doubt partly because of this, coupled with the fact that the authoress had British connections as a granddaughter to Queen Victoria, it sold extremely well. It was followed by a second Dulac collaborative title, Queen Marie's *The Stealers of Light* (1916). Here, however, Dulac perfectly visualised the text: 'Everything about her was white, glistening and shining; so shining that the human eye could hardly bear the radiance. Her long white hair hung about her; a circle of glow-worms surrounded her forehead.'

120 *Edmund Dulac's Picture-Book for the French Red Cross*

London: for *The Daily Telegraph* by Hodder and Stoughton, 1915
Private Collection

This was one of Dulac's best compilation volumes, which contained many of his favourite illustrations published again for the war effort. His strikingly simple Art Deco binding design gave style and elegance to an otherwise simple act of propaganda, which claimed rather grandly: 'There is not one penny that goes out of your pockets in this cause that does not bind France and Britain closer together.'

122 'Good Chiron taught his pupils to play upon the harp', 1937

Watercolour, signed

52 x 48 cm

Kendra and Allan Daniel Collection

By the early 1920s Dulac had given up his characteristic gift book illustrations as popular tastes changed. His book-buying public deserted him in favour of the slight productions emanating from the new age of the ephemeral. Commercial art work of any kind was in fact very hard to find, but fortunately in 1923 he received a financial lifeline from America, when he was commissioned to produce a series of eight to twelve annual colour cover designs for the American magazine, Hearst's *American Weekly*, the Sunday supplement of *The New York Weekly American*. At first he was allowed to choose his subjects and he took each series very seriously: 'Bible Scenes and Heroes', 'Characters from the Arabian Nights', 'Famous Vamps of History', 'Love Stories the Ancients believed in', or 'Enchanting Fairyland Lovers'. But in time, after arguments over production values and standards of popular taste, he considered the commission more of a chore than a happy collaboration. Nevertheless he persevered and produced over 100 designs, each drawn and painted with characteristic perfection. These designs also record the evolution of the Art Deco aesthetic into the late work of Dulac.

This rather risqué classical subject was published in the *American Weekly* on 4 April 1937 as part of Dulac's projected seven cover series of designs upon the theme of 'Beauty and the Beast', which also included 'The Maids of Athens and the Minotaur' and 'The Maid and the Unicorn'. In each he willingly borrowed from the strong element of neo-classicism found in the period's Art Deco style which dominated the entire series.

121 'Poland: A Nation', 1917

Colour lithograph

69.5 x 44.5 cm

© Copyright the Trustees of The British Museum

Published as one of a series of twelve poster designs – 'The Great War: Britain's Efforts and Ideals' (1917) – Dulac's bold conception joined with others by fellow artists Frank Brangwyn, Charles Shannon, William Nicholson, George Clausen and E. J. Sullivan which were produced for the Ministry of Information. Dulac was a dedicated war artist and he willingly provided several works for publications to aid the war effort. Here, in one of his most striking poster designs, he depicts in warm, rich colours a Polish warrior dressed in oriental-looking seventeenth-century armour, standing over the slain eagles of oppression, as the white eagle of liberated Poland rises up again to Freedom.

Kay Nielsen (1886–1957)

One of the most influential and colourful émigré gift book artists was the Dane Kay Rasmus Nielsen. The son of theatrical parents who instilled in him the love of fantasy and folklore, like many of his compatriots Kay Nielsen eventually flocked to London to try his luck with a portfolio of Beardsley-inspired drawings he hoped to exhibit there. His talent was immediately recognised and he was quickly taken up by Hodder and Stoughton to become their premier continental fantasist. Such was his remarkable talent that with just five published works of foreign folk and fairy tales he produced in Britain between 1912 and 1930 he still became a household name and he remains today a major influence upon the illustrated book.

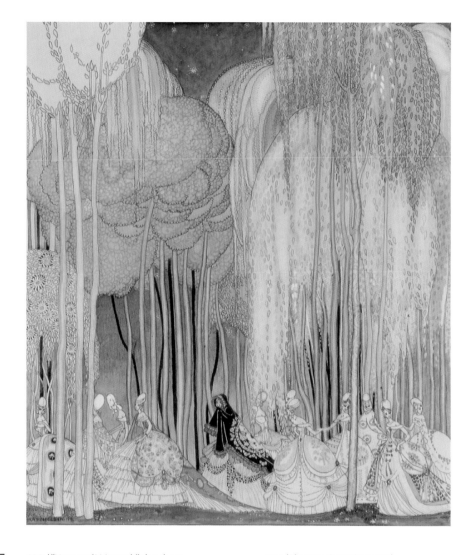

123 '"Your soul! My soul," they kept saying in hollow tones, according as they won or lost', for *In Powder and Crinoline*, 1912

Watercolour, pen and ink, heightened with gold
31.8 x 26 cm
Kendra and Allan Daniel Collection

This is one of several illustrations in Nielsen's first published book to betray a love of Beardsley's bizarre and challenging oriental aesthetic. Here, illustrating the tale 'John and the Ghosts', he created the necessary brooding atmosphere by exploring an elongated main figure, surrounded by bold, flat shadows to contrast with his eighteenth-century finery. It is a masterful pastiche of fashion and fear.

124 'The Dancing Princesses', for *In Powder and Crinoline*, 1912

Watercolour, signed
30 x 23 cm
Private Collection

Nielsen's first successful book, *In Powder and Crinoline* (1912), was a perfect showcase for his talents as a historicist. He delighted in creating textures and fine details borrowed from the past and the book remains one of the most theatrical of illustrated books.

125 'And flitted away as far as they could from the Castle that lay East of the Sun and West of the Moon' for *East of the Sun and West of the Moon*

London: Hodder and Stoughton, 1914
Private Collection

This is one of Nielsen's most famous images and one of the 25 he produced for this volume of Scandinavian folk tales. It illustrates the last prophetic line in the book. In clear homage to the Japanese prints he loved as a child, here Nielsen borrows from the Japanese woodblock print masters Hokusai and Hiroshige with his stylized water, and that strikingly spare oriental aesthetic of silhouetted branch and facetted rock.

126 '**The Faun**'

Watercolour, bodycolour,
heightened with silver and gold
37.5 x 24.8 cm
Kendra and Allan Daniel
Collection

This sylvan subject, inscribed
'Love's Faces II "The Faun"', was
probably intended for a periodical
illustration. Nielsen loved to
incorporate botanical themes into
his work. His beloved wife often
devoted herself to filling their tiny
California house with cheerful
arrangements to lift their spirits.

127 'Out of the fire jumped a little bird', from *Hansel and Gretel*, 1925

Watercolour, pencil, heightened with gold, signed
34.5 x 24.5 cm
Kendra and Allan Daniel Collection

This striking silhouette composition used the popular Danish paper cut-out style and illustrates the Grimm brothers' story of the Phoenix bird in 'The Juniper Tree', one of twelve colour plates Nielsen created for his final Hodder and Stoughton volume.

128 'Stop Prince, you cannot run away' for *Red Magic*, 1930

Gouache on paper, signed
27.5 x 19.5 cm
Kendra and Allan Daniel Collection

Nielsen's last published book was a poorly produced and truncated volume which, in content at least, celebrated his lifelong love of foreign folk tales. This was one of just eight colour plates with 50 pen and ink text drawings Nielsen created for *Red Magic: A Collection of the World's Best Fairy Tales from all Countries*, edited and arranged by Romer Wilson. It was issued by his new publisher Jonathan Cape in a red cloth trade edition only.

Alastair
(Hans Henning von
Voight; 1887–1969)

One of the most extraordinary characters of the period was the reclusive German artist Alastair, whose enigmatic pastiches of Beardsleyesque fantasy shocked and fascinated his British and American audiences. A master of pictorial effect which he devoted to the theme of decadence, in all its continental configurations, he created a small number of precious illustrated volumes which he filled with meticulous, bizarre ink drawings, costume designs and romantic narratives that brought the world of high eroticism once suggested by Beardsley into the twentieth century.

129 'The Insulting Bird', 1929

Pen and ink and watercolour
44.5 x 38 cm
Kendra and Allan Daniel Collection

Like his mentor Aubrey Beardsley, Alastair explored the intricacies of floral pattern and textures in his illustrations and costume designs. Here he created an emotive fantasy for an edition of the classic French erotic novel of libertines and lost innocence *Les Liaisons Dangereuses* (1929). Alastair worked intuitively and always set his illustrations 'by atmosphere and the persons – but not in a strict illustration of a scene described in the book'. Here he intended above all else to depict 'where everything is going against her and she begins to be rather nervous'.

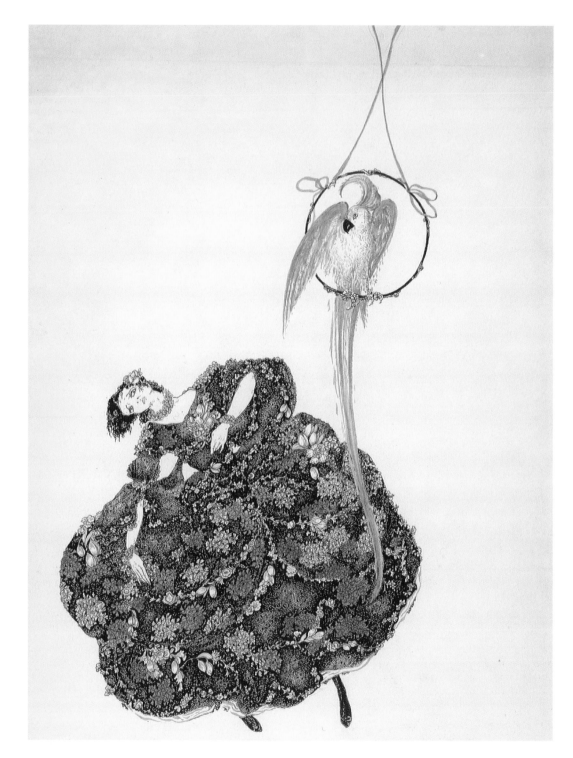

130 'Untitled' [A Dancer],
for *The Golden Hind*, Volume I,
October 1922

Pen and ink heightened with gold
on vellum
14.6 x 8.2 cm
Private Collection

This charming Art Deco flapper
appeared in the short-lived
periodical *The Golden Hind* in
October 1922 (Volume I, no. 1, p.
34), edited by Clifford Bax and
mystic and artist Austin Osman
Spare, published by subscription by
Chapman and Hall. The ill-fated
magazine had a small but
distinguished list of subscribers and
contributors including Spare, the
illustrators John Austin and Robert
Gibbings, and the painter Glyn
Philpot. Alastair's contributions were
few but memorable, including his
'Queen of the Night' series inspired
by Mozart's opera *The Magic Flute*.
Sadly, most of his work was poorly
reproduced and appeared too small
for a full appreciation of his
inimitable style.

131 **'Passionate Embrace',**
from *Manon Lescaut* **by the**
Abbé Prevost, 1928

London: John Lane; New York: Dodd,
Mead and Company, 1928
Collection of Dr Michael Richard
Barclay

This was one of Alastair's most
famously erotic costume
experiments in which a sensuous
Manon is swept off her feet, her
floral dress trailing into the
foreground and lowered to the small
of her back by her lover, whose head
nestles between her breasts. The
composition was a clear homage to
the inventiveness of Beardsley's
famous *Salome* drawing, 'The
Peacock Skirt' (cat. 4).

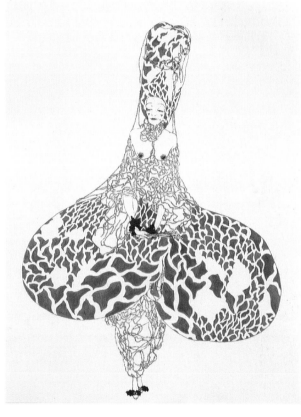

132 'Herodias' from *Salome*
by Oscar Wilde, 1925

Paris: G. Cres, 1925
Collection of Dr Michael
Richard Barclay

Herodius was Salome's infamous
mother and married to King
Herod, her former husband's
brother. Alastair created nine
illustrations to the French
edition of his favourite story, this
one an extravagant and
fantastical homage of Arabian
design to highlight the fate of
such a doomed character.

133 'Ashtaroth' from *The
Sphinx* by Oscar Wilde, 1920

London: John Lane, 1920
Collection of Dr Michael
Richard Barclay

Published in an edition of 1000
copies for which Alastair drew
20 illustrations, the story
haunted Alastair who executed
several sets of Sphinx drawings
in his lifetime. Ashtaroth was
the fertility goddess and
mother of the Canaanites and
the Phoenicians.

THE FANTASTIC BALLETS RUSSES

The Ballets Russes was founded by Sergei Diaghilev in 1909, and while it never performed in Russia, it quickly set innovative standards and became the pioneering dance and design company of the period, employing such dancers and choreographers as Pavlova and Nijinsky. Its set and costume designers included Leon Bakst, Braque, Picasso and Maurice Utrillo, while Debussy, Prokofiev, Ravel, Satie and Stravinsky worked as composers. Stravinsky's music for the 1911 production of *Petrushka* and Debussy's music for *L'après-midi d'un faune* combined with Leon Bakst's colourful costumes to become twentieth-century masterpieces. The company toured Europe, especially London and Paris, where many young artist-illustrators like Harry Clarke and Jessie King and their colleagues Ricketts, Dulac and Nielsen, and even the fairy lustreware ceramics designer Daisy Makeig-Jones, were so struck by their performances that they quickly adopted the colours and vibrant lines of these fantastical ballet productions.

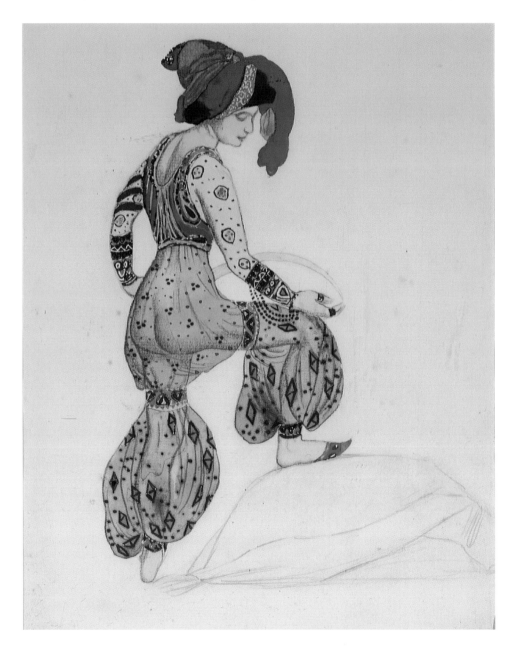

134 LEON BAKST

Costume design for 'The Blue Sultana' in *Scheherazade*, 1910

Watercolour and pencil, inscribed and signed on verso
29.5 x 23 cm
Private Collection

Famed for his orientalism, the Russian designer Leon Bakst (1866–1924) used peacock-hues and deep indigo here to a startling effect never before seen on the stage. *Scheherazade*, with music by Rimsky-Korsakov and choreographed by Michel Fokine, was produced at the Paris Opera House as a one-act drama on 4 June 1910. Even by standards of the period it was a racy subject for ballet: when the Shah, suspecting his favourite wife Zobeida of being unfaithful, pretends to go hunting, the ladies of his harem persuade the Great Eunuch to let in the black slaves and an orgy ensues, led by Zobeida and her favourite negro. The Shah returns and orders all executed, but passes over Zobeida, who then stabs herself to death before her husband.

135 LEON BAKST

Costume design for *La Peri*, 1911

Colour lithograph heightened with silver after the watercolour, signed and numbered 35/50
51 x 33 cm
Private Collection

Designed by Leon Bakst with a swirling scarf, peacock-hued ornaments and feather headdress, this is one of Bakst's masterpieces, used in the ballet *La Peri*, or 'The Flower of Immortality', originally created by Paul Dukas in 1912 for Nijinsky as Iskander. This was the haunting story of a rogue prince who steals the flower of immortality – an emerald-encrusted lotus – from the air spirit Peri, agent of good and beauty, but loses the flower and dies. The tale itself became legendary and had even been borrowed by Benjamin Disraeli, who wrote his own version in 1834. Moreover Bakst's designs were so popular that they were reproduced on Soviet propaganda porcelain in 1925, while this costume design print underwent a second printing of 100 copies, probably issued after the artist's death. The Ballets Russes had performed in London at the Coronation Season of Covent Garden in 1911, when Daisy Makeig-Jones was so dazzled by the colourful productions she returned to her studio intent upon imitating their brilliant colours.

136 CHARLES RICKETTS
Stage set design for *Montezuma*, c.1920

Watercolour
30.2 x 43.3 cm
Victoria and Albert Museum

Ricketts was encouraged by his young friend Cecil Lewis to write a dramatic version of Montezuma's last days, which inspired settings of brilliant colours boldly placed against atmospheric backgrounds to suggest the exoticism of South American art. Sadly the play was never produced, but it remained one of Ricketts's most colourful and favourite theatrical projects.

137 CHARLES RICKETTS
Design for the costume of *Montezuma*, c.1920

Watercolour
43.8 x 29 cm
Victoria and Albert Museum

ENCHANTMENT AT HOME

The demand for high-quality decorative design which might compete with the popular excesses of Art Nouveau and offer a refreshing new simplistic aesthetic was just one of the many elements of the early twentieth-century decorative arts. Inspired by the exoticism of the empire as well as the sleek lines, repetitive patterns and pure forms of a mechanical future, Art Deco was willingly embraced by the legions of middle-class households determined to make a statement. Much of the influence came from Europe, in particular Paris and Vienna, where the spare architectural aesthetic of the Secessionists appealed to a weary post-Edwardian world. Experts today in fact put the beginning of the Art Deco style at 1908–12, and, while it was not a rigid demarcation, the aesthetic survived until 1920, since its innovations were affected and prolonged by the First World War. By the late 1920s, with the advent of the Great Depression, the style turned more muted and subtle.

Daisy Makeig-Jones (1881–1945)

With the rise of women artists as craftswomen came a new generation of influential crafts and fine art designers, who left their mark upon their respective fields. One of the giants of British ceramics of the turn of the century was the redoubtable Daisy Makeig-Jones, a spirited Yorkshire lass who endured a restrictive training in the Wedgwood ceramics factory to become its leading figure and ultimately the firm's commercial saviour. Makeig-Jones's vision appeared in a line of fanciful bone china, 'Fairyland Lustre', which she craftily aimed at the aspiring, taste-conscious middle-class market, especially the homeowners searching for something special for their newly designed Art Deco drawing rooms. Inspired by Dulac and Nielsen illustrations, by the Ballets Russes and the legacy of Victorian fairyland, Makeig-Jones's body of tasteful fantasy ceramics set the highest standards and has become not only highly collectable today but remains extremely influential.

138 Vase 'Pillar' (Chinese fairies)

Bone china, printed in brown, painted in underglaze colours with sponged decoration and mother-of-pearl lustre glaze with gold print and edge
Height 54 cm, diameter 19.1 cm
Victoria and Albert Museum

This intricate design depicts the mountain palace of His Wang Mu, the Chinese Queen of the Fairies, which, according to legend, was nine storeys high and 333 miles in perimeter. The long staircase in one panel was irreverently labelled by Wedgwood factory workers as 'the Fire Escape'. The fairy in the swan flying boat was taken by Makeig-Jones directly from a much loved H. J. Ford illustration 'Flying Ship' for the fairy story 'Minnikin' in Andrew Lang's *Red Fairy Book* (1890).

139 Jar and cover 'Ghostly Wood' (Nursery fairies)

Bone china, printed in brown, painted in underglaze colours with sponged decoration and blue and orange lustre glazes with gold print and edges
Height 33.2 cm, diameter 26.3 cm
Victoria and Albert Museum

This charming design was discontinued in 1932, the year after Makeig-Jones's retirement. She freely adopted the original folk tale of 'The Legends of Croquemitane' (translated from the French in 1866), the story of Mitane, goddaughter of Charlemagne, who undertakes a journey through the fearsome 'Land of Illusion', peopled by lost souls, demon trees and ghastly apparitions, to conquer the 'Fortress of Fear'. Makeig-Jones's 'Land of Fear' included her own favourites like the White Rabbit from *Alice's Adventures in Wonderland*, the 'Fairy of the Desert' and 'Yellow Dwarf' from 'The Yellow Dwarf' by Madame d'Aulnoy, which had appeared in Andrew Lang's *Blue Fairy Book* (1889). One scholar has also suggested Gustave Doré's illustrations to *Croquemitane* were Makeig-Jones's source for the 'Roc' bird, toad, the 'Candle corpses' and the demon tree.

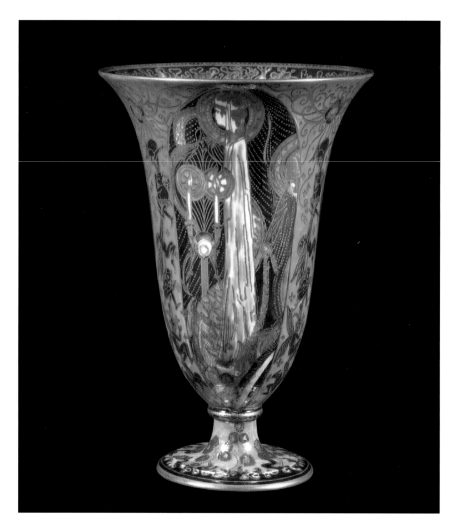

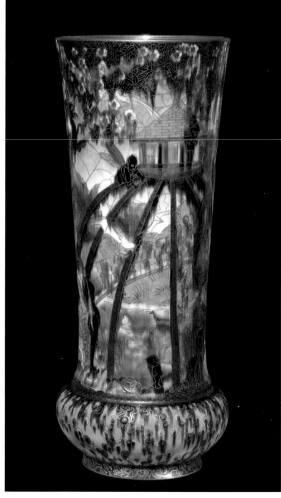

140 Vase 'Candlemass' (East of the Sun)

Bone china, printed in brown, painted in underglaze
colours with sponged decoration and mother-of-pearl
and mixed blue lustre glazes with gold print and edge
Height 21.5 cm, diameter 15.4 cm
Victoria and Albert Museum

This wonderfully inventive design based upon liturgical
and pagan rites was discontinued in 1926, but remains
one of Makeig-Jones's most successful fantasies. Based
upon the Christian church's festival of Candlemass
(2 February), which celebrates Christ's presentation at
the Temple 40 days after his birth, the custom was to
process holding candles and torches to mark the
occasion. Makeig-Jones mixed this religious theme with
pagan folklore, including the midsummer rite of rolling
a burning wheel downhill to determine the success of
the harvest. Her candle designs are greatly influenced
by Kay Nielsen's illustration of 'Prince Lindworm' from
East of the Sun, West of the Moon (1914).

141 Vase 'Imps on a Bridge' (Kewpie dolls)

Bone china, printed in brown, painted in underglaze
colours with sponged decoration and orange and
mother-of-pearl lustre glazes with gold print and edge
Height 43 cm, diameter 19 cm
Victoria and Albert Museum

The imps in this pattern were copied from the hugely
popular 'Kewpie' character invented by the American
artist Rose O'Neill, which first appeared in strip
cartoons in the American magazine *The Ladies' Home
Journal* in 1909, then became a manufactured doll
which was sold throughout the world throughout the
1920s. This popular pattern remained in production
from 1924 to 1941.

THE LURE OF EXOTIC EMPIRE

With the rise of the Modern Age, Britain's attitude towards its empire began to change. In time British imperialism gave way to a wider public understanding of the world, the Empire and its multifarious attractions. The British Commonwealth was coined in 1926, and throughout the 1920s artists, intent upon searching out new avenues of inspiration, turned to the exotic elements of Kipling's India or the magic of the Near and Far East. Travelling artists brought home landscapes as well as ideas inspired by these foreign lands and in turn they inspired the Art Deco interiors and salon exhibitions of modern Britain. One of the finest exponents of this 'Commonwealth School' was the multi-talented polymath artist Sir Frank Brangwyn, whose numerous landscapes, decorative murals, prints, ceramics and even furniture designs represented the ultimate in a career which spanned almost a century, and for the staggering accomplishments of which he was knighted.

Sir Frank Brangwyn, RA (1867–1957)

The largely self-taught Welshman Frank Brangwyn had the ability and the talent to spot a trend and develop it artistically. A student in William Morris's workshop, he graduated to Art Nouveau designs for Samuel Bing's legendary Parisian emporium, before abandoning the decorative arts for studio painting. He travelled extensively and recorded his travels, exhibiting at the Royal Academy at the astonishing age of eighteen. Spain, Italy and Africa beckoned and he spent a lifetime in the shadow of southern European aesthetics.

He is included here, however, for his ill-fated public works project, the House of Lords panels, which he intended to design as hymns to the glory of the British Commonwealth. The cult of the exotic which had so strongly infiltrated Art Deco Britain would have a high altar in these government-sponsored murals. Bright, colourful and exuberant, these panels would symbolise the age. Sadly their disastrous fate remained in the hands of a staid civil service which rejected them outright. However, they remain today as telling symbols of the exciting modernist aesthetic which had captivated the Age of Enchantment.

142 CLARICE CLIFF
'Life in a Tropical Forest', *c.*1935

Ceramic plaque after Brangwyn's designs for the British Empire Panels, House of Lords, London
Diameter 44 cm
Private Collection

One of four porcelain plaques produced to commemorate Brangwyn's ill-fated House of Lords panels, the design was adopted from Brangwyn's painting by the period's noted ceramic designer Clarice Cliff (1899–1972). She was artistic director of the Newport pottery, and had worked for the earthenware firm A. J. Wilkinson, where Brangwyn had also designed ceramics.

143 **Photograph of Frank Brangwyn painting the House of Lords panels in tropical designs in his studio,** *c.* 1930

12.5 x 15.5 cm
Private Collection

Brangwyn spent seven years designing and painting the 3000 square feet of mural panels for the House of Lords gallery. He rarely used studio assistants, preferring to work independently upon each enormous panel.

144 **Print cabinet and stand,** *c.* 1910

Cherry wood with coloured gesso decoration in imitation, with steel fittings of incised lacquer
173 x 136.5 x 83 cm
Victoria and Albert Museum

Brangwyn designed this cabinet for his own use in his studio at Temple Lodge, Hammersmith before he presented it to the museum in 1932. His love of things Italian is apparent in his choice of figures for the front panel while he attempted to imitate exotic Chinese lacquerware surfaces over the cherry wood structure. The cabinet was built by Paul Turpin.

Selected Bibliography

GENERAL READING

The 1890s: A Literary Exhibition, National Book League (catalogue), London, 1973

Art Nouveau, Museum of Modern Art (catalogue), New York, 1960

Christian, John, *The Last Romantics*, Barbican Art Gallery (catalogue), London, 1989

Clive, Mary, *The Day of Reckoning*, London, 1967

Duncan, Alastair, *Art Deco*, London 1988

The Edwardian Era, Barbican Art Gallery (catalogue), London, 1987

Felmingham, Michael, *The Illustrated Gift Book 1880–1930*, Scolar Press, London, 1989

Gaunt, William, *The Aesthetic Adventure*, London, 1945

Horne, Alan, *Dictionary of Twentieth Century British Book Illustrators*, Woodbridge, Suffolk, 1996

Houfe, Simon, *Fin de Siècle: The Illustrators of the Nineties*, London, 1992

Houfe, Simon, *Dictionary of Nineteenth Century British Book Illustrators*, Woodbridge, Suffolk, 1996

Jackson, Holbrook, *The Eighteen Nineties*, London, 1913

Johnson, Diana, *Fantastic Illustration and Design in Britain 1850–1930*, Rhode Island School of Design (catalogue), 1979

Lambourne, Lionel, *The Studio: High Life and Low Life*, Victoria and Albert Museum (catalogue), London, 1993

Lost Paradise: Symbolist Europe, Montreal Museum of Fine Art (catalogue), Montreal, 1995

Peppin, Bridget, *Fantasy*, London, 1975

Peppin, Bridget and Lucy Mickelthwait, *Dictionary of British Book Illustrators: The Twentieth Century*, London, 1983

Rheims, Maurice, *Art Nouveau*, London, 1966

Sketchley, R. E. D., *English Book Illustration of Today*, London, Reprinted 1966

Sturgiss, Matthew, *Passionate Attitudes*, London, 1995

Taylor, John Russell, *The Art Nouveau Book in England*, London, 1966

Thorpe, James, *English Illustration of the Nineties*, London, 1935

BIBLIOGRAPHY OF ARTISTS

The following selected list of books, monographs and catalogues is intended to introduce the artists and does not claim to be definitive. Monographs are given precedence over short articles or reviews in periodicals.

ALASTAIR (Hans Henning von Voight)

Arwas, Victor, *Alastair: Illustrator of Decadence*, London, 1979

Crosby, Harry (introduction), Alastair's illustrated edition of Oscar Wilde's *The Birthday of the Infanta*, Paris, 1928

Ross, Robert (introduction), *Alastair: Forty-Four Drawings in Colour and Black and White*, John Lane, London and New York, 1914

Symons, Arthur (introduction), Alastair's edition of Edgar Allan Poe's *The Fall of the House of Usher*, Paris, 1928

Van Vechten, Carl (introduction), *Fifty Drawings by Alastair*, New York, 1925

AUBREY BEARDSLEY

Aubrey Beardsley, Tokyo Shimbun (catalogue), Tokyo, 1983

Brophey, Bridget, *Black and White: A Portrait of Aubrey Beardsley*, London, 1968

Clark, Kenneth, *Beardsley and his World*, London, 1976

Clark, Kenneth, *The Best of Beardsley*, London, 1979

Easton, Malcolm, *Aubrey and the Dying Lady*, London, 1972

Engen, Rodney, *Beautiful Decadence*, Tokyo Shimbun (catalogue), Tokyo, 1998

Gallatin, A. E., *Aubrey Beardsley: A Catalogue of Drawings*, New York, 1945

Hind, C. L., *The Uncollected Work of Aubrey Beardsley*, London, 1925

Lasner, Mark Samuel, *A Selective Checklist of the Published Work of Aubrey Beardsley*, Boston, 1995

Maas, Henry (editor), *The Letters of Aubrey Beardsley*, London, 1970

Macfall, C. H., *Aubrey Beardsley: The Clown, the Pierrot of his Age*, New York, 1927

Reade, Brian, *Aubrey Beardsley*, London, 1967

Reade, Brian, *Aubrey Beardsley: An Exhibition at the Victoria and Albert Museum* (catalogue), London, 1966

Reade, Brian, *Beardsley Re-mounted*, London, 1989

Reid, Aileen, *Beardsley*, London, 1991

Ross, Robert, *Aubrey Beardsley*, London, 1909

Sturgiss, Matthew, *Aubrey Beardsley: A Biography*, London, 1998

Walker, R. A., *Aubrey Beardsley Miscellany*, London, 1949

Weintraub, Simon, *Beardsley*, New York, 1967

Wilson, Simon, *Beardsley*, Oxford, 1976

SIR FRANK BRANGWYN, RA

Belleroche, William de, *Brangwyn's Pilgrimage*, London, 1948

Brangwyn, Rodney, *Brangwyn*, London, 1978

Galloway, Vincent, *The Oils and Murals of Sir Frank Brangwyn, RA*, (F. Lewis Ltd), 1962

Horner, Libby and Gillian Naylor, *Frank Brangwyn*, Leeds City Art Gallery, Leeds, 2006

Liss, Paul, *Frank Brangwyn*, Fine Art Society (catalogue), London, 2006

Macer-Wright, Philip, *Brangwyn: A Story of Genius at Close Quarters*, London, 1940

Shaw-Sparrow, Walter, *Frank Brangwyn and His Work*, London, 1910

HARRY CLARKE

Bodkin, Thomas, 'The Art of Mr Harry Clarke', *The Studio*, Volume 79, Number 320

Bowe, Nicola Gordon, *Harry Clarke*, Douglas Hyde Gallery (catalogue), Dublin, 1989

Bowe, Nicola Gordon, *Harry Clarke: His Graphic Art*, Mountrath, Co. Laois, Ireland, 1983

Bowe, Nicola Gordon, *The Life and Work of Harry Clarke*, Dublin, 1989

The Stained Glass of Harry Clarke, Fine Art Society (catalogue), London, 1988

EDWARD JULIUS DETMOLD AND CHARLES MAURICE DETMOLD

Alfrey, Nicholas and Richard Verdi, *The Detmolds* (catalogue), York, 1983

The Art Journal, 1908, pp. 186 and 224

A Collection of Watercolours by Edward Julius and Charles Maurice Detmold, The Keyser Gallery (catalogue), Cirencester, Gloucestershire, 4–25 October 1979

Dodgson, Campbell, 'Maurice and Edward Detmold', *The Print Collector's Quarterly*, December 1922, pp. 373–405

Dodgson, Campbell, 'The Recent Etchings of Edward Detmold', *Art Work*, I, No. 3, February–April 1925, pp. 145–51

'Modern Etchers: No. 8 E. J. Detmold', *Walker's Monthly*, August 1928, pp. 3–4

'Mr E. Detmold's Drawings', *The Athenaeum*, 13 November 1909, p. 597

Nicholson, Keith, *The Fantastic Creatures of E. J. Detmold*, London, 1976

Nicholson, Keith, 'Edward Julius Detmold, Illustrator Extraordinaire', *Antiquarian Book Monthly Review*, Vol. 2, No. 9, issue 19, September 1975, pp. 12–16

Spielmann, M. H., 'Two Boys – Maurice and Edward Detmold', *Magazine of Art*, 1900, pp. 112–18

The Studio: 'Studio Talk', 1904, p. 252; 1905, p. 80; 1906, p. 244; also T. Martin Wood, 'A note on Mr Edward J. Detmold's Drawings and Etchings of Animal Life', 1911, pp. 289–97; 'Reviews and Notices', 1913, p. 178; April 1929, p. 228; June 1932, p. 363

Unpublished MS biography of Ian MacPhail; also his introduction to the Folio Society's *Jungle Book*, 1994

EDMUND DULAC

Edmund Dulac, Hartnoll & Eyre Ltd (catalogue), London, December 1970

Hughey, Ann Connolly, *Edmund Dulac: His Book Illustrations*, Potomac, Maryland, 1995

Larkin, David (editor), *Dulac*, London, 1975

Peppin, Bridget, *Fantasy*, London, 1975

White, Colin, *Edmund Dulac*, London, 1976

Wilenski, R. H. (introduction), *Edmund Dulac Memorial Exhibition*, Leicester Galleries, London, 1953

ANNIE FRENCH

Christian, John, *The Last Romantics*, Barbican Art Gallery (catalogue), London, 1989, p. 202

Cullen, Anthea, *Angel in the Studio*, London, 1979, p. 223

LAURENCE HOUSMAN

Engen, Rodney, *Laurence Housman*, Stroud, England, 1983

Graves, Richard Perceval, *A. E. Housman, the Scholar Poet*, London, 1981

Housman, Laurence, *The Unexpected Years*, London, 1937

Housman Society Journal, Street, England, 1977

The Housmans, National Book League (catalogue), London, 1975

The Laurence Housman Collection of Ian Kenyur-Hodgkins (catalogue), Church Enstone, England, 1978

Pugh, John, *Bromsgrove and the Housmans*, London, 1974

Taylor, John Russell, *The Art Nouveau Book in England*, London, 1966

JESSIE MARION KING

Jessie M. King, Barclay Lennie Fine Art (catalogue), Glasgow, 1989

Jessie M. King and E. A. Taylor, Sotheby's (catalogue), Glasgow and London, 1989

Scottish Arts Council, *Jessie M. King* (catalogue), Glasgow and London, 1971–72

Taylor, E. A., 'Miss Jessie M. King', *The Booklover's Magazine*, Edinburgh, 1904 (reprinted in the *IBIS Journal*, 2005)

White, Colin, *Jessie M. King*, Edinburgh, 1990

White, Colin, 'Bookplate Designs of Jessie M. King', *The Bookplate Journal*, Vol. 13, No. 1, March 1995, pp. 3–29

DAISY MAKEIG-JONES

Batkin, Maureen, *Wedgwood Ceramics 1846–1959*, Richard Dennis (catalogue), London, 1982

Fontaines, Una des, *Wedgwood Fairyland Lustre: The Work of Daisy Makeig-Jones*, London, 1975

Fontaines, Una des and Lionel Lambourne, *Miss Jones and her Fairyland*, Victoria and Albert Museum (catalogue), London, 1990

Makeig-Jones, Daisy, 'Some Glimpses of Fairyland', Josiah Wedgwood & Sons Ltd, 1921

KAY NIELSEN

Johnson, Diana, *Fantastic Illustration and Design in Britain 1850–1930* (catalogue), Rhode Island, 1979, pp. 78–79

Larkin, David (editor), *The Unknown Paintings of Kay Nielsen*, London, 1977 (with eulogy by Hildegarde Flanner)

Nicholson, Keith, *Kay Nielsen*, London, 1975

Pottarnees, Welleren, *Kay Nielsen: An Appreciation*, Green Tiger Press, 1976

WILLY POGANY

Horne, Alan, *Dictionary of Twentieth Century British Book Illustrators*, Woodbridge, Suffolk, 1996

Houfe, Simon, *Dictionary of Nineteenth Century British Book Illustrators*, Woodbridge, Suffolk, 1996

IBIS (Imaginative Book Illustration Society) *Newsletter*, No. 1, London, Autumn 1995

IBIS Journal No. 1, 'Aspects of Illustration', London, 1999

Junior Book of Authors, New York, 1954

Peppin, Bridget and Lucy Mickelthwait, *Dictionary of British Book Illustrators: The Twentieth Century*, London, 1983

Reed, Walt and Roger, *The Illustrator in America*, New York, 1984

ARTHUR RACKHAM, RI

Baugham, Roland, *The Centenary of Arthur Rackham's Birth*, Columbia University Library, New York, 1967

The Bookman, London, December 1910, pp. 141–42; October 1925, p. 7; October 1926, p. 11

Croykendall, Frederick, *Arthur Rackham: A List of Books Illustrated by Him*, New York, 1922

Darrell, Margery (editor), *Once Upon a Time: The Fairy Tale World of Arthur Rackham*, London, 1972

Edwards, Barbara (née Rackham), 'Try to Look Like a Witch', *Columbia Library Columns*, New York, May 1968, pp. 3–7

Engen, Rodney, *Arthur Rackham*, Dulwich Picture Gallery (catalogue), London, 2002

Gettings, Fred, *Arthur Rackham*, London, 1975

Hamilton, James, *Arthur Rackham*, London, 1990

Hamilton, James, *Arthur Rackham*, Sheffield City Art Galleries (catalogue), Sheffield, 1979

Hartrick, A. S., 'Arthur Rackham: An Appreciation', *Old Watercolour Society's Club*, 1933–34, pp. 51–52

Hudson, Derek, *Arthur Rackham: His Life and Work*, London, 1960

Latimore, S. B. and G. C. Haskell, *Arthur Rackham: A Bibliography*, London, 1936

CHARLES RICKETTS, ARA

Art for All (The Ricketts and Shannon Collection in the Fitzwilliam Museum (catalogue), Cambridge, 1979

Barclay, Michael, *Catalogue of the Works of Charles Ricketts, RA, in the Carlisle Museum and Art Gallery* (catalogue), Stroud, England, 1985

Calloway, Stephen, *Charles Ricketts, Subtle and Fantastic Decorator*, London, 1979

Darracott, Joseph, *The World of Charles Ricketts*, London, 1980

Delaney, J. G. P., *Charles Ricketts*, Oxford, 1989

French, Cecil, 'The Wood Engravings of Charles Ricketts', *Print Collectors' Quarterly*, Vol. 14, 1927, pp. 191–217

Moore, T. Sturge, *Charles Ricketts, RA*, London, 1933

CHARLES ROBINSON, RI

Freitas, Leo de, *Charles Robinson*, London, 1976

Robinson, William Heath, *My Line of Work*, London, 1938

[S. E. B.], 'A New Book Illustrator: Charles Robinson', *The Studio*, V, 1895, pp. 146–50; also VI, 1896, pp. 191–92

Watson, A., *The Savage Club: a Medley of History, Anecdote and Reminiscence*, London, 1907

SIDNEY SIME

Emanuel, Frank L., 'Our Graphic Humourists: Sidney Sime', *Magazine of Art*, February 1904

Heneage, Simon and Henry Ford, *Sidney Sime: Master of the Mysterious*, London, 1980

'The Published Drawings of Sidney Sime', *IBIS Newsletter*, London, Winter 1998, pp. 21–39

Lawrence, Arthur, 'Apotheosis of the Grotesque', *The Idler*, Volume 12, January 1898, pp. 755–66

Macfall, Haldane, 'The Genius of Sidney Sime', *Illustrated London News*, November 1922

'Hal Dane' [Haldane Macfall], 'Some Thoughts on the Art of S. H. Sime', *Saint Paul's*, September 1899

Sidney H. Sime Exhibition, St George's Gallery (catalogue), London, 1927

Skeeter, Paul W., *Sidney H. Sime, Master of Fantasy*, Pasedena, California, 1978

Swaffer, Hannen, 'Sime: the Prophet in Line', *The Graphic*, November, 1922

BERNARD SLEIGH

Christian, John, *The Last Romantics*, Barbican Art Gallery (catalogue), London, 1989, pp. 112–13

Peppin, Bridget and Lucy Mickelthwait, *Dictionary of British Book Illustrators: The Twentieth Century*, London, 1983, p. 279

Sleigh, Bernard, *Memoirs of a Human Peter Pan* (unpublished MS in the Birmingham Public Library)

Index

Note: References are to page numbers. Those in **bold** figures indicate catalogue plate pages. [fig.] indicates a figure illustration within the essay section.

A

Abel, Monsigneur 58
Académie Julian 37, 40
Aladdin 43
Alastair 7, 24, 35, 44–45, [fig. 19], 118, 144, **144–47**
  Fall of the House of Usher 45
  Fifty Drawings 45
  Forty-three Drawings 45
  The Golden Hind **145**
  Les Liaisons Dangereuses 45, **144**
  Manon Lescaut 45, **146**
  Masque of Queen Bersabe 45
  Picture of Dorian Gray 45
  Salome 45, **147**
  Sebastian Von Storck 45
  The Sphinx 45, **147**
Albert, Prince 26, 46, 49, 101
Altdorfer, Albrecht 30
American Weekly 36, 40, 139
Andersen, Hans 22, 24, 26, 30, 40, 42, 43
  Fairy Tales 24, 43, 102
  Stories 38
  Thumbelina 47
Anning Bell, Robert 32
Arabian Nights 7, 22, 43
Aristophenes 14
  Lysistrata 14
Art Deco 21, 36, 37, 40, 43, 47, 77, 139, 151, 153
The Art Journal 25
Art Nouveau 31, 100-01, 151
L'Art Nouveau (Paris) 48
Arts and Crafts Movement 11, 26, 48, 52
Ashdowne Park, Sussex 25
Austin, John 145

B

Bakst, Leon 14, 19, 21, 24, 28, 39, 45, 46, **148–49**
  Cinderella 46
  The Magic Flute 46
  La Peri 46, **149**
  Scheherazade 46, **148**
  Sleeping Beauty 46
Ballets Russes 14, 19, 26, 28, 39, 45–47, 118, 148, **148–49**, 151

Balzac, Honore 12
Barbirolli, Sir John 50
Barker, Harley Granville 130
Barlow, Jane 67
Barrie, J. M. 26
  Peter Pan 26, 30, 31, 89
Bartolozzi, Francesco 64
Baudelaire, Charles 10, 14
Bax, Clifford 145
Bayeuth, Germany 21
Beardsley, Aubrey 4, 7, 10, 11, 12–15, 17, 18, 19, 20–24, 27–29, 30–32, 34, 37, 40, 42, 44–46, 52, **55**, **57–58**, **60–65**, 78, 82–83, 96, 98, 140, 144
  'The Abbe' **2**, **163**
  Davidson's *Plays* **62**
  Mademoiselle de Maupin 58, **65**, 79
  Le Morte Darthur 13, 21, 30, 55, **60**
  The Rape of the Lock 24, **64**
  The Story of Venus and Tannhauser **63**
  Under the Hill 63
  Volpone 58, **65**, 79
Beardsley, Mabel 62
Beerbohm, Max 14
Belgian Symbolism 29
Benois, Alexander 45
Bernhardt, Sarah 21
Bible 22
Bilibin, Ivan 45
Bing, Samuel 48
Bodley Head see John Lane
Bosch, Hieronymous 30
Botticelli, Sandro 12, 29
Bottomley, Gordon 21
Braque, Georges 45, 148
Brangwyn, Sir Frank 48–50, 139, 153, **153–54**
  The Arabian Nights 48
  British Empire Exhibition 48–49
  Don Quixote 48
  House of Lords panels [fig. 20], 49–50, **153–54**
  The Rubaiyat of Omar Khayyam 48
Brangwyn Hall, Swansea 50
British Commonwealth 153
British Empire 10, 24, 48–50, 153
British Empire Exhibition 48–49
Burne-Jones, Sir Edward 12, 13, 34

Burton, Sir Richard 22
The Butterfly 22

C

Caffyn, W. H. **66**
Campbell, Mrs Partrick 14
Cape, Jonathan 43, 143
Carlyle, Thomas 30
Carroll, Lewis 30
  Alice in Wonderland 36, 116
Celtic 23–25, 29
Chapman and Hall 145
Chartres cathedral 24
Chelsea Arts Ball 40
Chelsea School of Art 46
China 11, 37, 39, 40, 42, 47, 52, 55, 154
Christensen, Arthur 43
Clarke, Harry 10, 23–25, [fig. 10], 26, 28, 29, 42, 45, 78, **82–88**, 114, 132, 148
  Andersen's *Fairy Tales* 24
  Perrault's *Fairy Tales* 24
  Goethe's *Faust* 24
  Poe's *Tales of Mystery and Imagination* 24, **86**
  The Rape of the Lock **82–85**
  Selected Poems of Swinburne 24
  The Years at the Spring 24, **87**
Clausen, George 139
Cliff, Clarice 50, **153**
Coalport (china) 46
Collarossi Academy 40
Cottingley fairy hoax 27
Country Life 33

D

Dadd, Richard 26
Daily Mail Ideal Home Exhibition 50
La Dame aux Camélias 12
Daumier, Honore 30
Davos, Switzerland 25, 88
Davidson, John 63
  Plays 62, 93
Debussy, Claude 30, 148
Delville, Jean 29
Dent, J. M. 13, 27, 30, 33, 37, 95
Detmold Brothers 7, 23, 25, 33–35, 50, **56**, 108, **108–17**
  'The Hornbill' 34, **109**
  Kipling's *The Jungle Book* 25, 34, **110–11**
  'Peacocks' 34, **56**
  Pictures from Birdland 33–34
Detmold, Charles Maurice 33–34, **109**, **110**, **111**

Detmold, Edward 33–35, **108–17**
  The Arabian Nights 35, **111**
  Birds in Town and Village 35
  The Fables of Aesop 35
  Fabre's *Book of Insects* 33–35
  Greater Things and a Greater than Things 35
  Life 35
  The Life of the Bee 33, 35
  Second Jungle Book 35
  Selflessness 35
  Twenty-four Nature Pictures 33, 35
Diaghilev, Sergei 14, 45–47, 148
The Dial 10
Disney, Walt 7, 26, 43–44
Discovery Magazine 39
Disraeli, Benjamin 26, 149
Dodgson, Campbell 34
Doges Palace, Venice 50
The Dome 26
Doré, Gustave 22, 151
Dowdeswell Galleries, London 42
Doyle, Sir Arthur Conan 23, 27, 89
Doyle, Richard 26–27, 47
Dukas, Paul 149
Dulac, Edmund 7, 17, 23, 24–26, 30–31, 33, 35–36, [fig. 17], 42, 43, 45, 47, 50, **73**, 118, 120, **120–39**, 148, 151
  American Weekly series 40, 139, **139**
  The Bells **8**, 38, 130, **132**, **133**
  Cathay Pacific lounge 40
  'Circe' **front cover**, **129**
  The Dreamer of Dreams **138**
  Dulac's *Fairy Book* 38, 39
  Dulac's *Picture-Book for the Red Cross* 39, **138**
  The Golden Cockerell 40
  King Albert's Book 39
  Jane Eyre 37
  'Macbeth' **130**
  'Poland: A Nation' **139**
  Princess Badoura 38, **135**
  Princess Mary's Gift Book 39
  The Rubaiyat of Omar Khayyam 38
  Sinbad the Sailor 38, 39, **136**, **137**
  The Sleeping Beauty **128**, 129
  Stories from Hans Andersen 38, **131**
  Stories from the Arabian Nights 17, 37–39, **120–23**, 135

The Tempest **125–26**
Dumas, Alexandre 129
Dunsany, Lord 22–24, 78
  The Gods of Pegana 22
  Time and the Gods 22
Durer, Albrecht 18, 20, 30, 33, 34

E

Elgar, Sir Edward 33
Elizabeth II, Queen 40
Empress of Britain (ship) 40
English Art Club 34
Ernest Brown and Philips *see* Leicester Galleries
Erte (Romain de Tirtoff) 24
Eureka 21, 22, 79
Evans, Frederick H. 57, **57**
Everyman 43
Exposition de l'Art pour l'Enfance, Paris [fig. 12], 95

F

Fairyland Lustre (china) 47–48, **47–48**, 151, **152**
Fine Art Society, London 34
Fitzgerald, John Anster 26
Fokine, Michel 148
Forbes, Stanhope 98
Ford, Henry J. 47, 151
Forster, E. M. 25, 46
  A Room with a View 46
France, Anatole 33
Fra Angelico 14
Franco-British Exhibition 48
French, Annie 7, 24, 29, 46, 89, 90, **96**, **97**
  'The Daisy Chain' **96**
  'Fairies' Invitation' 29
  'A Fairy Tale' **96**
  'The Floral Dress' 29
  'The Lace Train' 29
  'The Plumed Hat' 29
  'The Unhappy Prince' 29
  'The Queen and the Gypsies' **97**
French Symbolism 10
Fry, Roger 14
Fuller, Loie 101
Fuseli, Henry 22

G

Galsworthy, John 46
  Forsyte Saga 46
Gaskin, Arthur 26
Gautier, Theophile 14
  Mademoiselle de Maupin 14, **65**
Genée, Adeline 62

George V, King 48
Gibbings, Robert 145
Glasgow School style 27–29, 90, 96
Glasgow School of Art 27, 29, 89, 90
Godwin, E.W. 52, 55
Goethe, Johann Wolfgang von 24
  Faust 24, 119
The Golden Hind 145, **145**
Gosse, Edmund 32
Gowans and Gray, Glasgow 28
Grahame, Kenneth 32, 33
  The Wind in the Willows 32–33
The Graphic 23
Great Exhibition of 1851 46
Greenaway, Kate 12
Gregoire, Emile 31, 101
  'Captivity' 101
  'Undine' **101**
Grieg, Edvard 40
Grimm Brothers 30, 128
  Fairy Tales 30, 31

H
Hardy, Thomas 130
Harland, Henry 62
Harrap, George 24, 35, 118
Harris, Sir Augustus 62
Hawthorne, Nathaniel 119
Hearst, William Randolph 22, 36, 40, 139
  American Weekly 36, 40, 139
Heine, Heinrich 40
High Victorian Gothic 46
Hiroshige, Ando 141
Hodder and Stoughton 35, 37, 42, 43, 121, 125, 128, 129, 133, 135, 138, 140, 143
Hoffman, Joseph 37
Hogarth, William 14
  'The Rake's Progress' 14
  'Marriage a la Mode' 14
Hokusai, Katsushika 23, 141
Holbrooke, Joseph 23
G. L. Holtegaard Museum, Copenhagen 44
Houghton, Arthur Boyd 16, 72
Housman, A. E. 15, 19, 33
  A Shropshire Lad 17
Housman, Clemence 15–16, 18, 66, **70–71**, 72
Housman, Laurence 9, 10, 13, 15–19, 20, 30, 31, **66–72**, 135
  A Farm in Fairyland 17
  All Fellows 17, [fig. 5], 19
  Arabian Nights Re-told 17
  The Blue Moon 17, **72**
  The End of Elphintown 16, [fig. 3], 63, **67**

The Field of Clover 17, [fig. 6], [fig. 7], **69**, **70**
Goblin Market 16, [fig. 4], **66**, 99
Green Arras 19
The House of Joy 17, **67**
The Little Flowers of St Francis 66
Of the Imitation of Christ **71**
The Pageant **68**
Pre-Raphaelitism in Art and Poetry 9
The Sensitive Plant 19
Seven Legends of Lower Redemption 19
Thompson's *Poems* 17
Hudson, W. H. 35
Hughes, Arthur 16
Huysmans, Joris-Karl 10, 24
  A Rebours 10, 12, 57

I
Ibsen, Henrik 40
The Idler 14, 21, 22, 79
Illustrated London News 23, 50, 127
L'Illustration 127
Impressionism 11
International Exhibition, London 34
Irish Celtic Revival 23
Irish Renaissance 23
The Irish Statesman 25
The Irish Times 24
Iveagh, Lord 49

J
James, Henry 32
Japanism 11–13, 19–20, 25, 29, 33, 37, 39–40, 52–53, 141
Jerome, Jerome K. 21
John, Augustus 23
Jones, Paul (café) 29
Jonson, Ben 14
  Volpone 14, 58, 65, 79

K
Kandinsky, Wassily 14
Keats, John 28
Kegan Paul, Routledge 67
Kempis, Thomas a 71
  Of the Imitation of Christ 71, **71**
King, Jessie Marion 7, 24, 26, 27–29, [fig. 11], 42, 45, 46, 89, 90, **90–95**, 96, 148
  'All the Day's Filled with Sunshine' 29
  The Book of Bridges 28
  'Cinderella' 27
  'The Cricket' 29
  The Defence of Guenevere and Other Poems 28, **95**

'The Enchanted Faun' **94**
Everyman 28
The Flowers of Parnassus 28
'The Forsaken Merman' 27
The High History of the Holy Graal 27, **95**
'The House with the Evil Eyes' 29
Nursery and doll's house designs [fig. 12], **95**
Our Trees and How to Know Them 28
'The Sea Voices' 29, **93**
'Sing Out for the Happy You Feel Inside' 29
Kipling, Rudyard 25, 98
  The Jungle Book 25, 34–35, 108, **110**, **111**
  Puck of Pook's Hill 98
Klee, Paul 14
Knopf, Alfred 45

L
Ladies' Home Journal 152
Lambeth School of Art, London 15, 19, 30
Lane, John 10, 11, 13, 14, 16, 17, 28, 32, 45, 66, 95
Lang, Andrew 47, 151
  Colour Fairy Books 47
Larche, Raoul 31, **101**
  'The Pool' 101
  'The Sirens" **101**
Laurens, J. R. 40
de Lautrec, Gabriel 14
Le Gallienne, Richard 62
Leicester Galleries, London (also as Ernest Brown and Philips) 24, 31, 37, 43, 114, 129
Leighton, Sir Frederic (later Lord) 13, 17, 20, 66, 74
Leno, Dan 21
Lewis, Cecil 150
Lewis, C. S. 31
Leyland, Frederick 55
Liberty's, London 29, 46
Limited Editions Club, New York 40
London Zoo 50
Louis IV, King 10

M
Macdonald, Francis 27, **90**
Macdonald, Margaret 27, 46, 90
Machen, Arthur 23
  The Hill of Dreams 23
  The House of Souls 23
  The Three Imposters 23
Mackintosh, Charles Rennie 27, 37, 90
Maclise, Daniel 49

Macmillan, George 17
MacNair, Herbert 27, 90
Madame Bovary 12
Mademoiselle de Maupin 14, 65, **65**
Maeterlinck, Maurice 28, 33
  The Blue Bird 80
  The Life of the Bee 33
Magazine of Art 108
Makeig-Jones, Daisy 46–48, 148–49, 151, **151–52**
  Fairyland Lustre (china) 47–48, **151–52**
Malory, Thomas 13
  Le Morte Darthur 13, 21, 30, 55, **60**
Manon Lescaut 12, 45
Mantegna, Andrea 12, 58
Menton, France 14, 58
Meryon, Charles 23
Metropolitan Opera, New York 36
Meynell, Alice 15
Miller, Arthur 44
Milton, John 28
Minton (china) 46
Mir Iskustva (The World of Art) 46
Moreau, Gustave 20, 21, 24
  'Salome' 24
Morris, William 13, 19, 28, 48, **53**, 60, 67
  The Defense of Guenevere 28, **95**

N
National Observer 33
National Trust 33
Nevinson, C. R. 49
Newbury, Francis 29
Newlyn School 98
New Republic 26
New York Bookman 32
New York Times 14
New York World 13
Nicholson, William 25, 139
  'Peter Pan' stage designs 26
  The Un-Common Cat 25
Nielsen, Kay 7, 23, 24, 26, 35, 37, 39, 40–45, 50, 51, 118, 140, **140–43**, 148, 151
  The Arabian Nights 43, 45
  'The Book of Death' 42
  East of the Sun, West of the Moon 42, 47, **141**, **152**
  'Fantasia' 43
  'The First Spring' 44
  Hans Andersen's *Fairy Tales* 43
  Hansel and Gretel 42, 43, **143**
  In Powder and Crinoline **6**, 24, 42, **56**, **140**

King Albert's Book [fig. 18]
'The Little Mermaid' 44
Red Magic 43, **143**
Snow White 43
Nielsen, Ulla 43
Nijinsky, Vaslav 45, 148–49
Nordau, Max 15
  Degeneration 15

O
Old London Bridge 49
O'Neill, Rose 152
  'Kewpie doll' 152
Orpen, Sir William 24

P
The Pageant 68, 76
Pall Mall Budget 30
Pall Mall Gazette 21, 22
Pater, Walter 45
Pavlova, Anna 148
Perrault, Charles 24, 90, 128
  Fairy Tales 24
  'The Sleeping Beauty' **92**
Piazza, Henri 127
  L'Illustration 127
Phillpott, Eden 79
Philpot, Glyn 145
Picasso, Pablo 14, 45, 148
Pick-Me-Up 21
Pierrot 42, 45
Piranesi, Giovanni 23
Poe, Edgar Allan 22–24, 82, 87, 130
  The Bells 38, **132–33**
  The Fall of the House of Usher 45
  'The Moon' 22
  Tales of Mystery and Imagination 24, 31, **86**
The Poet's Dream (Danish play) 43
Pogany, Willy 23, 24, 26, 29, 35–37, [fig. 15], [fig. 16], 39, 42, 178, **118–19**
  Alice in Wonderland 36
  The Children in Japan 36
  Lohengrin **118–19**
  The Rime of the Ancient Mariner 36, [fig. 16]
  The Rubaiyat of Omar Khayyam 35–37, 118
  'Rumpilstilskin' **119**
Pope, Alexander 14
  The Rape of the Lock 14, 24, 64, **82–85**
Poulsen, Johannes 43
Pre-Raphaelites 9, 16, 18–19, 20, 23, 29, 68, 72, 76, 105
Prevost, Abbe 45
  Manon Lescaut 45
Prokoviev, Sergei 45, 148

Q

Quiller-Couch, Sir Arthur 42,
128

R

Rackham, Arthur 7, 23–26,
30–32, [fig. 13], 33, 37–40,
42–43, 47, **98–100**, 101,
102, 114, 120, 132
Aesop's *Fables* 31
Goblin Market 31, **99**
Grimm's *Fairy Tales* 30–31
Gulliver's *Travels* 30
The Ingoldsby Legends 30
A Midsummer Night's Dream
31
Mother Goose 31
Peter Pan 30, 31, 37
The Rhinegold and the Valkerie
31, **100**
Rip Van Winkle 30
*Siegfried and the Twilight of the
Gods* 31
*Tales of Mystery and
Imagination* 31
Undine 31, 101
'The Widow Whitgift' 31, **98**
The Wind in the Willows 32
The Rape of the Lock 14, 24, **64**,
82–85
Ravel, Maurice 45, 148
Reinhardt, Max 43
Reiniger, Lotte 37
Rhead, George Wooliscroft 29
Ricketts, Charles 10, 11, 16,
19–21, [fig. 8], 26, 30, 32, 39,
46, 66–67, 71, **73–77**, 130,
148, **150**
Beyond the Threshold 21, **77**
'Cupid and Psyche' 20, **76**

The Mikado 21
Montezuma **150**
'Oedipus and the Sphinx' 20,
74
The Sphinx 20–21, **75**
Rimsky-Korsakov, Nikolai 148
Robinson, Charles 23, 26,
32–33, 102, **102–07**
Aladdin **103**
Bee 33, **105**
The Big Book of Fairy Tales 103
A Child's Garden of Verses 32
The Goldfish Bowl **106**
The Happy Prince 33, **105**
The Sensitive Plant 33, [fig. 14],
104
'The Siesta' **107**
'The Spotted Mimulus' 32,
102
Robinson, Thomas 32
Robinson, William Heath 7, 23,
32, 33, 43, 102
Hans Andersen's Tales 43
The Twelfth Night 125
Ross, Robert 45
Rossetti, Christina 17, 31
Goblin Market 17, 31, **99**
Rossetti, Dante Gabriel 16, 17,
55, 99
Routledge, George 28 (*see also*
Kegan Paul)
Royal Academy, London 29, 30,
33, 34, 48
Royal Copenhagen Theatre 43
Royal Doulton (china) 48
Royal Fine Arts Commission
50
Royal Glasgow Institute 29
Royal Institute of Painters in
Watercolour 33–34

Royal Society of Painter Etchers
34
Royal Watercolour Society 30
Ryder, Knight 22, 78

S

Satie, Eric 45, 148
The Savoy 14
Scaramouche (play) 43
Shakespeare, William 20, 30, 31,
88, 98, 125, 130
A Midsummer Night's Dream 31
The Tempest **125–26**
Shannon, Charles 16, 19, 30, 39,
68, 73, 75, 139
Shaw, George Bernard 19
Shealing Atelier, Paris 24, 28
Shelley, Percy Bysshe 19
The Sensitive Plant 19, 33,
[fig. 14], **104**
Shepard, Ernest Howard 7
Sibelius, Jean 43
Sime, Sidney 7, 10, 21–23,
[fig. 9], 24, 29, 50, **78–81**
The Bogey Beasts 23, 80
'The Felon Flower' 22, **78**
'The Great God Pan' 21
'The Incubus' 22
'The Mermaid" 21, 22, **79**
'The Sime Zoology' 23, **80**
Sixties School of Illustration 16,
72
The Sketch 23, 80
Sleigh, Bernard 26–27, **89**
Ancient Mappe of Fairyland 26
The Coming of the Fairies 27
A Faerie Calendar 26
A Faerie Pageant 26
'The Horns of Elfland Faintly
Blowing' **89**

Memoirs of a Human Peter Pan
26, 89
Smith, W. H. 14
Smithers, Leonard 65
Spare, Austin Osman 145
Spenser, Edmund 26, 28
Spielmann, M. H. 108
'The Spooks' 27, 90
Stevenson, Robert Louis 32
Stravinsky, Igor 45, 148
Petrushka 45, 47
Strindberg, August 42
The Studio 10, 13, 24, 27, 32, 61,
93
Sullivan, E. J. 139
Sunday Express 50
Symbolism 20, 23, 24, 29, 74

T

The Tatler 23, 80
Taylor, Ernest Archibald 24,
27–29, **90**
Templeton, James (rugs) 50
Tennyson, Alfred 28
Thompson, Francis 17
Poems 17
The Times (London) 13, 18, 33, 35
Tintoretto 50
Tolkien, J. R. R. 7
The Lord of the Rings 7
Torquay School of Art 46
Toulouse-Lautrec, Henri 59
Turin Exhibition of Decorative
Art 27
Turpin, Paul 154

U

Undine 26, 31, 101
Utamaro, Kitagawa 11
Utrillo, Maurice 45, 148

V

Vale Press 20, 73, 76
Vechten, Carl Van 45
Venetian Carnevale 13
Verlaine, Paul 40
Victoria, Queen 9, 26, 31, 101, 138
Vienna Secessionists 151
Volpone 14, **65**

W

Wagner, Richard 20, 31, 32, 98,
100–02, 118
Waldron, Laurence 82
Warner's First National Studios
(film) 36
Wedgwood (china) 46–48, 151
Westminster Fire Office 30
Westminster Gazette 30
Weyhe Gallery, New York 45
Whistler, James McNeill 11, 52,
55
'Peacock Room' 11, [fig. 1]
Wilde, Oscar 10–12, 14–15, 17,
19, 55, 57, 62
The Happy Prince 33, **105**
A House of Pomegranates 28
The Picture of Dorian Gray 10,
45, 57
Salome 11, 13, 45, **55**, **147**
The Sphinx 11, 20, 21, 45, **75**,
147
Wilkinson, A. J. (china) 48, 153
Williams, Ralph Vaughan 33
Wilson, Romer 43, 143
Wright, Frank Lloyd 90

Y

Yeats, William Butler 39
The Yellow Book 10, 13, 14, 17,
26, **59**, 62

ARTISTIC COPYRIGHTS

PHOTOGRAPHIC CREDITS